WHERE WE GO FROM HERE

ALSO BY BERNIE SANDERS

Bernie Sanders Guide to Political Revolution
Our Revolution
The Speech
Outsider in the House

BERNIE SANDERS

Where We Go from Here

TWO YEARS IN THE RESISTANCE

Thomas Dunne Books St. Martin's Press New York

THOMAS DUNNE BOOKS.
An imprint of St. Martin's Press.

www.thomasdunnebooks.com
www.stmartins.com

Designed by Steven Seighman

The Library of Congress Cataloging-in-Publication Data
is available upon request.

ISBN 978-1-250-16326-4 (hardcover)
ISBN 978-1-250-16327-1 (ebook)

Our books may be purchased in bulk for promotional, educational,
or business use. Please contact your local bookseller or the Macmillan Corporate
and Premium Sales Department at 1-800-221-7945, extension 5442,
or by email at MacmillanSpecialMarkets@macmillan.com.

First Edition: November 2018

10 9 8 7 6 5 4 3 2 1

This book is dedicated to my family—my wife, Jane, my brother, Larry, and my children, Levi, Heather, Carina, and Dave, and their spouses. It is also dedicated to my grandchildren, Sunnee, Cole, Ryleigh, Grayson, Ella, Tess, and Dylan—and all the children of the world. Our struggle is for them, and we cannot fail.

CONTENTS

CONTENTS

CONTENTS

ACKNOWLEDGMENTS

Let me applaud the millions of Americans who, over the last two years, have struggled in the resistance to maintain the American ideals of democracy, justice, and decency. Keep fighting. Let me also thank my Senate and campaign staffs for all their hard work in helping to advance the political revolution. Finally, let me express my appreciation to Ari Rabin-Havt and Warren Gunnels for their assistance on this book.

WHERE WE GO FROM HERE

INTRODUCTION

During my campaign for president in 2016, I stated over and over again that the future of our country was dependent upon our willingness to make a political revolution. I stressed that real change never occurs from the top down. It always happens from the bottom up. No real change in American history—not the labor movement, the civil rights movement, the women's movement, the gay rights movement, the environmental movement, nor any other movement for social justice—has ever succeeded without grassroots activism, without millions of people engaged in the struggle for justice.

That's what I said when I ran for president. That's what I believe now. That's what I've been working to accomplish over the last several years. At a time of massive and growing income and wealth inequality, as our nation moves closer and closer to an oligarchic form of society, we need an unprecedented grassroots political movement to stand up to the greed of the billionaire class and the politicians they own.

And the good news is, we're making progress. People in every region of our country are standing up and fighting back against the most dishonest and reactionary president in the history of the Republic. In state after state they are also taking on establishment politicians who are more concerned about protecting their wealthy campaign contributors than they are with the needs of the middle class and the working people they are supposed to represent.

We're making progress when millions of people, in every state in the country, take to the streets for the Women's March in opposition to Trump's reactionary agenda. We're making progress when an unprecedented grassroots movement elects a young African American as mayor of Birmingham, Alabama. We're making progress when tens of thousands of Americans turn out at rallies and town hall meetings to successfully oppose the Republican efforts to throw thirty-two million people off health insurance. We're making progress when governors and local officials announce, in response to student demands, tuition-free public colleges and universities. We're making progress when over the past two years hundreds of first-time candidates from every conceivable background run for school board, city council, state legislature, and Congress—and many of them win.

The good news is that the American people are far more united than the media would like us to believe. They get it. They know that over the last forty years, despite a huge increase in worker productivity, the middle class has continued to shrink, while the very rich have become much richer. They know that, for the first time in the modern history of the United States, our kids will likely have a lower standard of living than us.

The bad news is that instead of going forward together, demagogues like Trump win elections by dividing us. The bad news is that too many of us are getting angry at the wrong people. It was not an immigrant picking strawberries at $8 an hour who destroyed the economy in 2008. It was the greed and illegal behavior of Wall

Street. It was not transgender people who threw millions of workers out on the street as factories were shut down all across the country. It was profitable multinational corporations in search of cheap labor abroad.

Our job, for the sake of our kids and grandchildren, is to bring our people together around a progressive agenda.

Are the majority of people in our country deeply concerned about the grotesque level of income and wealth inequality that we are experiencing? You bet they are. Do they believe that our campaign finance system is corrupt and enables the rich to buy elections? Overwhelmingly, they do.

Do they want to raise the minimum wage to a living wage and provide pay equity for women? Yes, they do. Do they think the very rich and large corporations should pay more in taxes so that all of our kids can have free tuition at public colleges and universities? Yup. Do they believe that the United States should join every other major country and guarantee health care as a right? Yes, again. Do they believe climate change is real? You've got to be kidding. Are they tired of the United States of America, the wealthiest country in the history of the world, falling apart at the seams, with roads, bridges, water systems, wastewater plants, airports, rail, levees, and dams either failing or at risk of failing? Who isn't?

Further, a majority of the American people want comprehensive immigration reform and a criminal justice system that is based on justice, not racism or mass incarceration.

Today, what the American people want is not what they are getting. In fact, under Republican leadership in the House, Senate, and White House, they are getting exactly the opposite of what they want.

The American people want a government that represents all of us. Instead, they are getting a government that represents the interests and extremist ideology of wealthy campaign contributors. They want environmental policies that combat climate change and pollution and that will allow our kids to live on a healthy and habitable planet. Instead, they are getting executive orders and legislation that push more fossil fuel production, more greenhouse gas emissions, and more pollution. They want a foreign policy that prioritizes peacemaking. Instead they are getting increased military spending and growing hostility to our long-term democratic allies. They want a nation in which all people are treated with dignity and respect, and where we continue our decades-long struggle to end discrimination based on race, religion, gender, sexual orientation, and nation of origin. Instead, they have a president who seeks to win political support by appealing to those very deep-seated prejudices.

During the last several years, I've worked hard in Washington, but I have also traveled to thirty-two states in every region of our country. I have seen the beauty, strength, and courage of our people. I have also seen fear and despair.

I have talked to people with life-threatening illnesses in West Virginia who worry about what will happen to them, or their loved ones, if they lose the health insurance that keeps them alive. I have talked to young immigrants (Dreamers) in Arizona who are frightened to death about losing their legal status and being deported from the only country they have ever known. I have talked to a young single mom in Nevada worried about how she can raise her daughter on $10.45 an hour. I have talked to retirees and older workers in Kansas who are outraged that, as a result of congressional legislation, they could lose up to 60 percent of the pensions they paid into and were promised as deferred compensation for a lifetime of work. I have talked to senior citizens in Vermont who divide their pills in half because they are unable to afford the outrageously high cost of prescription drugs. I have talked to workers in San Francisco who, as a result of gentrification, are no longer able to live in the neighborhoods they grew up in and love. I have talked to family members around the country who have lost loved ones to the opioid and heroin epidemics sweeping the nation.

I would hope that each one of us honors the men and women who have, throughout history, put their lives on the line to defend our country. I will never forget meeting, in a small town in northern Vermont, an older gentleman who was part of the D-Day invasion at Normandy. I had goose bumps talking to him, trying to imagine all that he had gone through and the extraordinary sacrifices he and his comrades made.

In school, we teach our kids to understand and appreciate the sacrifices that veterans made in defending "our way of life." But we spend too little time explaining to them what that "way of life" means.

Standing in Gettysburg in November 1863, soon after that terrible battle that claimed tens of thousands of casualties, Abraham Lincoln reminded his compatriots, and all of us, what that "way of life" was, and what our enduring responsibility in a democratic society is. He stated ". . . that we here highly resolve that these dead shall not have died in vain—that this nation, under God, shall have a new birth of freedom, and that government of the people, by the people, for the people, shall not perish from the earth."

Government of the people, by the people, for the people. Creating a nation that works for all, and not just the few. That was worth fighting for in 1863. It is worth fighting for today.

Maintaining a vibrant democracy based on principles of justice has never been easy. In these dangerous and unprecedented times, it may be more difficult than ever.

As a result of the disastrous *Citizens United* Supreme Court decision, billionaires are now able to spend hundreds of millions of dollars anonymously in ugly TV ads demonizing candidates who dare to stand up to them. Republican governors and legislatures are working overtime to suppress the vote, making it harder for people of color, poor people, and young people to vote.

The internet and social media now allow for the worldwide transmission of total lies, and the capability of targeting those lies to susceptible populations.

Further, recent studies show what the average American has long known. More and more mainstream media political coverage is devoted to gossip and issues of personality, and less and less to the major problems facing our country and the world. During the last presidential campaign, for example, there was almost no discussion devoted to climate change, the greatest environmental crisis facing our planet. There was hardly a mention that, in the wealthiest country in the history of the world, 40 million Americans live in poverty, or that we have the highest rate of childhood poverty of nearly any major country on earth.

Yes, I know. These are painful and frightening times. Many friends have told me that they dread reading the papers or watching TV. But let us be clear. Despair is not an option. This struggle is not just for us. It is for our kids, our grandchildren, and the future of the planet.

This book is about some of what I and millions of progressives have been trying to accomplish day by day over the last several years.

Some of that work took place inside the Beltway, and much of it outside the Beltway. But no matter where it took place, the goal has always been the same. We must create a vibrant democracy where the voices of all people are heard. We must build a nation that leads the world in the struggle for peace, and for economic, social, racial, and environmental justice. And we must unite our country while repairing the damage Trump has done trying to divide us up.

The struggle continues.

MEETING WITH HILLARY CLINTON

My campaign was over. With the completion of the DC primary on June 14, 2016, the Democratic presidential primary process had finally come to an end. Starting from nowhere, with a relatively unknown senator from a small state, our campaign had taken on virtually the entire Democratic establishment, shocked the political world, and helped transform American politics.

Starting off at about 3 percent in the polls, we ended up winning twenty-two states and received over 13 million votes. We showed that working people all over this country were prepared to support an agenda that stood up to the billionaire class and that called for the transformation of our economic and political life.

Most significantly, we had won overwhelming support from the young people of our country—black, white, Latino, Asian American, and Native American. This was the future of our country, and we ended up winning more votes from people under forty than Clinton and Trump combined. Young people had shown very clearly that they were tired of status quo politics and were prepared to accept a very new vision of what our country could become.

I was extremely proud that a poll conducted by the Harvard Institute of Politics suggested that our campaign had fundamentally changed the way that millennials think about politics. John Della Volpe, who conducted the poll, stated, "He's not moving a party to the left. He's moving a generation to the left."

Despite losing 95 percent of the establishment superdelegates to Clinton, we won 1,846 delegates to the Democratic Convention.

With no super PAC or dependence on wealthy donors, we had also revolutionized campaign fund-raising. We received some 8 million individual contributions, from over 2 million people, more than any candidate in American history, averaging $27. Hundreds of thousands of volunteers played an active role in our grassroots campaign in every state, and we drew to our rallies some of the largest crowds in recent political history.

On the night of June 14, with the primary process over, Hillary Clinton and her key advisers John Podesta and Robby Mook sat down in a Washington, DC, hotel with my campaign manager, Jeff Weaver, my wife, Jane, and me. The purpose of the meeting was to discuss the best way forward and to determine how we could most effectively work together to defeat Trump.

Coming into the meeting, I had a number of questions on my mind. In order to gain the support and enthusiasm of people who had voted for me, was Secretary Clinton willing to move closer to some of the popular positions that I had advocated during the campaign? Could we work together to write a progressive Democratic Party platform that made it crystal clear that we stood with the working families of our country? Could we begin the process of changing some of the archaic and antidemocratic rules of the Democratic Party and open the party up to working people and young people who currently felt little or no allegiance to it?

Those were some of my concerns. Clinton, legitimately enough, had other and more immediate interests. She wanted to know what kind of role I was prepared to play in the general election. When and how should I endorse her? What states would be best for me to focus on? How could we best work together at the convention in Philadelphia?

As is always the case, the devil was in the details. After reaching a general agreement at the meeting as to the best path forward, we trusted our staffs to work out the particulars over the next several weeks.

THE MOST PROGRESSIVE POLITICAL PLATFORM IN U.S. HISTORY

I have said it a million times, but I think it bears repeating. The campaign that I ran for president was never about me. It wasn't about political gossip, campaign strategy, the horse race, or fundraising.

The campaign was about creating a government and an economy that works for all of us, not just the top 1 percent. While the primaries were over, the fight for economic, racial, social, environmental, and political justice was not—not by a long shot.

As part of the political revolution, our next mission was to write the most progressive platform in the history of the Democratic Party: a platform that would live on beyond the campaign, and, more importantly, a platform that would serve as a beacon for Democratic candidates at the federal, state, and local levels. This would be a document that stated loudly and proudly what the Democratic Party was supposed to stand for.

Historically, the Democratic Party's platform has been crafted largely behind closed doors, deep inside the corridors of the Democratic National Committee (DNC), by the staff of the presidential nominee. The final product is usually heavy on empty rhetoric but light on specific policy solutions. After the convention, the platform is forgotten about—and sits on a shelf somewhere, collecting dust.

We set out to change all of that, in terms of both process and content. After all, the 13 million Americans who voted for our campaign did not do so because of my good looks, my hair, or my charming personality. Well, maybe a few of them voted for my hair. But most of them supported me because of the issues I stood for, and because they were sick and tired of a political and economic system that was rigged to benefit those on top and was being held in place by a corrupt campaign finance system.

Shaping a platform for a political party when you didn't win the nomination is not an easy task. The last runner-up in the Democratic primaries to contest the writing of the Democratic platform was Jesse Jackson, in 1988. Reverend Jackson ran an extraordinary and historic campaign that year, one that not only changed the nature of politics in America but helped create a new multiracial progressive movement. During his campaign, Jackson won nearly 7 million votes. I was proud to endorse his campaign and happy that he won the Vermont primary that year. Unfortunately, however, very few of his progressive positions were incorporated into the Democratic Party platform of 1988.

But this was not 1988. This was the year 2016, and something extraordinary had happened—something that, frankly, I had not anticipated. Millions of Americans had stood up and demanded fundamental changes in our economic and political life. Their voices could not be ignored, and the Democratic leadership understood that.

Our staff began to negotiate with the Clinton campaign and the DNC on how the platform would be written, who would write it, what would be included in it, and how it could be amended.

After a lot of back-and-forth, we agreed that there would be a platform-writing subcommittee comprising fifteen voting members and two nonvoting members. Our campaign would select five of the voting members, the Clinton campaign would choose six, and the rest would be chosen by the DNC. Maya Harris, Clinton's senior policy adviser, and Warren Gunnels, my policy director, would be nonvoting members.

This subcommittee would be in charge of holding hearings, writing the first draft of the platform, amending it in St. Louis, and sending it to the full 187-member platform committee, which would meet in Orlando on July 8 and 9.

The DNC picked Representative Elijah Cummings of Maryland to chair the subcommittee. Elijah is a friend of mine, and an outstanding member of Congress. His selection as chair was an encouraging sign.

For our representation on the subcommittee, I picked Representative Keith Ellison, the co-chair of the Congressional Progressive Caucus; Bill McKibben, the founder of 350.org and a leading champion in the fight against climate change; James Zogby, the founder of the Arab American Institute; Dr. Cornel West, one of the most important philosophers of our time; and Deborah Parker, a progressive leader in the Native American movement.

Clinton's team picked Representative Luis Gutiérrez; Paul Booth, with the American Federation of State, County and Municipal Employees (AFSCME); Carol Browner, President Bill Clinton's Environmental Protection Agency (EPA) administrator; Wendy Sherman, the lead negotiator of the Iran nuclear deal;

Neera Tanden, president of the Center for American Progress; and Ohio state representative Alicia Reece.

The DNC's final three members were Representative Barbara Lee; Bonnie Schaefer, the former CEO of Claire's Stores; and former Representative Howard Berman, now a lobbyist with the Motion Picture Association of America.

Even though the Sanders faction was in the minority and we could not pass any of our amendments on our own, the Clinton team and the DNC representatives negotiated in good faith. The goal was for both campaigns to work together to bridge many of the policy issues that had divided us during the election.

Did we come to an agreement on everything? Of course not. I was disappointed that, among other issues, the Clinton and DNC delegates opposed our amendments to enact Medicare for All, ban fracking, and oppose the job-killing Trans-Pacific Partnership.

But we made major strides forward.

The platform included the initiative I worked on with Clinton to make public colleges and universities tuition-free for families making $125,000 or less and to substantially reduce student loan debt. This proposal, if enacted into law, would revolutionize higher education in this country.

It also included another policy I worked on with Clinton, one that called for doubling the funding for community health centers. This initiative would increase primary care, including mental health care, dental care, and low-cost prescription drug access for an additional 25 million people.

While we weren't able to include Medicare for All, Clinton's team did include a public option to allow everyone in this country to participate in a public insurance program and to allow Americans between the ages of fifty-five and sixty-four to opt in to

Medicare. These ideas had been killed by then-Senator Joe Lieberman and the insurance industry during the consideration of President Obama's health care program.

During the proceedings in St. Louis and Orlando, we were victorious in including amendments in the platform that made it the policy of the Democratic Party to fight for:

- A $15-an-hour federal minimum wage indexed to inflation;
- Breaking up too-big-to-fail banks and passing a twenty-first-century Glass-Steagall Act;
- Levying a tax on carbon, methane, and other greenhouse gas emissions to aggressively combat climate change;
- Making massive investments in wind, solar, and other renewable energy;
- Requiring Medicare to negotiate for lower prescription drug prices and making it legal to import safe and affordable medicine from Canada and other countries;
- Abolishing the death penalty, ending mass incarceration, and enacting major criminal justice reforms;
- Establishing a path toward the legalization of marijuana;
- Expanding Social Security by increasing taxes on those making over $250,000 a year;
- Preventing employers from cutting the earned pension benefits of more than 1.5 million Americans;
- Closing loopholes that allow corporations to stash their cash offshore to avoid paying taxes, and using the revenue generated by this policy to create millions of jobs rebuilding our crumbling infrastructure;
- Making it easier for workers to join unions through majority card-check recognition and by ensuring a first contract through binding arbitration;

- Ending disastrous deportation raids, banning private prisons and detention centers, and passing comprehensive immigration reform;
- Moving to automatic voter registration and the public financing of elections, making Election Day a federal holiday, eliminating super PACs, and passing a constitutional amendment to overturn *Citizens United*; and
- Creating the most comprehensive agenda ever to protect and expand the rights of Native Americans and indigenous communities.

All of these progressive policies were at the heart of our campaign, and I was very proud of the accomplishment of our platform-writing team. I also appreciated the willingness of the Clinton team and the DNC to work with us and create a platform that we could all be proud of.

Normally, the media doesn't pay much attention to the writing of a party platform. This time, it was different. This platform, and the process by which it was written, generated a whole lot of attention.

As NBC News headlined: "Democrats Advance Most Progressive Platform in Party History."

They reported: "The draft platform . . . showed Sanders' clear influence. The document goes further left than Clinton's position on a number of issues, with Sanders policy director Warren Gunnels saying his campaign achieved 'at least 80 percent' of what it came for. 'I think if you read the platform right now, you will understand that the political revolution is alive and kicking,' he said."

NBC also reported: "Clinton won the nomination and now effectively controls the party, but it was Sanders who drove the process in Orlando. While many questioned his decision to stay in the primary race long after losing the nomination, none of the progress of his ideas on the platform would have happened if he had dropped out."

The media often worries about personality, gossip, polling, and gaffes. I worry about ideas and policy that will improve the lives of the working families of our country. The Democratic platform of 2016 is a very good blueprint for how we can do that. I am confident that the ideas expressed in that document will not be forgotten. They will, in fact, become the heart and soul of a growing progressive movement.

July 26, 2016

THE DEMOCRATIC CONVENTION

On July 26, 2016, in a prime-time speech at the Democratic National Convention in Philadelphia, I endorsed Hillary Clinton and urged my supporters and the American people to elect her as president.

A few weeks earlier, appearing with Secretary Clinton before a packed audience in Portsmouth, New Hampshire, I said, "Secretary Clinton has won the Democratic nominating process. She will be the Democratic nominee for president, and I intend to do everything I can to make certain she will be the next president of the United States."

The Democratic Convention in Philadelphia, attended by delegates from fifty states, territories, the District of Columbia, and Democrats Abroad, was tumultuous and, for me, quite emotional. On a personal level, it was an extraordinary experience to come face-to-face with the 1,846 Sanders delegates from every state in the country who had put their hearts and souls into the campaign and who had worked day and night to elect me president. I was truly overwhelmed by their support and affection.

And I was so proud of them. Black, white, Latino, Asian American, Native American, gay, and straight—they embodied what must become the future of American politics. Anyone looking at our supporters could see in a moment that they were not the traditional Democratic politicians who attend conventions. They were not superdelegates. They were not political insiders. They were not wealthy. They were not governors or members of Congress. They were not well connected or movers and shakers in their own states. And they weren't cynical.

These people were bold progressives who had a new vision for America and were the face of the political revolution. They had taken on the political establishment back in their own states and won the right to be a Sanders delegate at the convention. Many of them were young, electoral politics was new to many of them, and for the vast majority, this was the first political convention they had ever attended. Some of them were so strapped financially that the campaign had to establish a scholarship fund to pay their transportation costs to Philadelphia.

The now-famous DNC emails that we later learned were stolen by hackers working for a Russian intelligence agency had been released at the start of the convention. The content of these emails, which were not a shock to me, showed that the leadership of the DNC had tilted the playing field during the primary in favor of Hillary Clinton's campaign. As a result, the chair of the DNC, Debbie Wasserman Schultz, was forced to resign. Many of my delegates, who were not great fans of Hillary Clinton or the Democratic establishment to begin with, were further enraged.

My view, ever since the presidential primary had ended, was not complicated. Trump was an unmitigated disaster—a racist, sexist bigot and xenophobe who had to be defeated. He was also a phony and a pathological liar who had preyed on the fears of the American people.

Now, with the primaries behind us, it was clear to me that the progressive community had to go forward in three areas. First, we had to fight for the most progressive Democratic platform that we could—a platform that incorporated as much of our campaign agenda as possible. This was important not just for the presidential campaign but for congressional and Senate races as well.

Second, we had to defeat Trump and elect Hillary Clinton. This to me was a no-brainer, and I had a hard time understanding how anyone could disagree. I was, perhaps, more aware than anyone of Secretary Clinton's political deficiencies. I had spent a year pointing them out. But I was also aware that, on her worst day, she would be a better president than Trump on his best day. We simply did not have the luxury of sitting back and allowing a mean-spirited authoritarian billionaire to become president.

Third, we had to build on the grassroots momentum of the campaign, continue the political revolution, and bring more and more people into the political process. Unlike many other presidential candidates who had lost their elections, I did not intend to fade away into the sunset. We had brought new progressive ideas into the mainstream and had been enormously successful in engaging millions of people in democracy. We were not going to give up. This campaign had never been about me alone. It was about the future of the country—and that struggle had to continue after the election. We were about more than a political campaign. We were about building a movement.

In terms of supporting Clinton, not all the Sanders delegates agreed with me. In a speech to my supporters at the beginning of the convention, I was booed by some for urging them to vote for her. My response was to speak to as many state delegations as possible to make the case for what I thought was obvious.

As Sam Frizell, of *Time* magazine, reported:

> *Amid fears that Bernie Sanders' delegates would again seek to disrupt proceedings on the floor of the Democratic Convention on Tuesday, the Vermont senator visited with state delegations to Philadelphia to corral them into supporting Hillary Clinton and calm their anger before the gavel opens the convention again.*
>
> *Sanders' effort was part of a full-court press to unify the Democratic Party after a fractious showing on Monday night, when booing, dissent and angry Sanders delegates stole the spotlight from much of the convention proceedings. "It is easy to boo," Sanders told the California delegation on Tuesday morning in central Philadelphia ahead of a roll call vote on the convention floor. "But it's harder to look your kids in the face who would be living under Donald Trump."*

While there were some vocal dissenters, most of my delegates agreed with the sentiments of Donna Smith, executive director of Progressive Democrats of America, a group that had been with me from the earliest days of the campaign, when she said, "I accept that electing Hillary Clinton is better than electing Donald Trump. I accept that."

Before the voting on the floor took place, I visited delegations from New York, California, Kansas, Wisconsin, and Alaska, among others. The point that I made over and over again was that we had to unite to defeat Trump. As *Time* magazine reported, I told the New York delegation, "There is no debate that we must defeat the worst Republican candidate in the modern history of this country."

I went on to point out that our "first task" was to elect Clinton. And our second task was to "continue the political revolution."

In addition to all of the politics in Philadelphia, Jane and I had a rare opportunity to spend time with much of our family. All four of my kids, Levi, Heather, Dave, and Carina, were at the convention, as were most of the grandchildren. I was especially delighted that my brother, Larry, whom I owed so much to, was able to come over from his home in Oxford, England, with my nephew Jacob.

Larry had worked hard in the Democrats Abroad organization, where we won the majority of votes. As a delegate, he was able to cast his vote before the entire convention. In a very moving moment, with tears in his eyes, Larry voted for me and invoked the memory of our parents, Eli and Dorothy Sanders. He said, "They did not have easy lives and they died young. . . . They loved the New Deal of Franklin Roosevelt and would be especially proud that Bernard is renewing that vision. It is with enormous pride that I cast my vote for Bernie Sanders."

I was also proud that my own small state of Vermont, where I had won 86 percent of the vote in the primary, was able to play an outsized role at the convention. At the end of the state voting, the chair of the Vermont delegation allowed me to nominate Hillary Clinton by acclamation.

Here is the speech that I gave at the Democratic National Convention on July 26, 2016, endorsing Hillary Clinton for president:

Good evening.

How great it is to be with you tonight.

Let me begin by thanking the hundreds of thousands of Americans who actively participated in our campaign as volunteers. Let me thank the two and a half million Americans who helped fund our campaign with an unprecedented

8 million individual campaign contributions—averaging $27 apiece. Let me thank the 13 million Americans who voted for the political revolution, giving us the 1,846 pledged delegates here tonight—46 percent of the total. And delegates: Thank you for being here, and for all the work you've done. I look forward to your votes during the roll call on Tuesday night.

And let me offer a special thanks to the people of my own state of Vermont who have sustained me and supported me as a mayor, congressman, senator, and presidential candidate. And to my family—my wife, Jane, four kids, and seven grandchildren—thank you very much for your love and hard work on this campaign.

I understand that many people here in this convention hall and around the country are disappointed about the final results of the nominating process. I think it's fair to say that no one is more disappointed than I am. But to all of our supporters—here and around the country—I hope you take enormous pride in the historical accomplishments we have achieved.

Together, my friends, we have begun a political revolution to transform America, and that revolution—our revolution—continues. Election Days come and go. But the struggle of the people to create a government which represents all of us and not just the 1 percent—a government based on the principles of economic, social, racial, and environmental justice—that struggle continues. And I look forward to being part of that struggle with you.

Let me be as clear as I can be. This election is not about, and has never been about, Hillary Clinton, or Donald Trump, or Bernie Sanders, or any of the other candidates who sought the presidency. This election is not about political gossip. It's not about polls. It's not about campaign strategy. It's not about fund-raising. It's not about all the things the media spends so much time discussing.

This election is about—and must be about—the needs of the American people, and the kind of future we create for our children and grandchildren.

This election is about ending the forty-year decline of our middle class and the reality that 47 million men, women, and children live in poverty. It is about understanding that if we do not transform our economy, our younger generation will likely have a lower standard of living than their parents.

This election is about ending the grotesque level of income and wealth inequality that we currently experience, the worst it has been since 1928. It is not moral, not acceptable, and not sustainable that the top one-tenth of 1 percent now own almost as much wealth as the bottom 90 percent, or that the top 1 percent in recent years has earned 85 percent of all new income. That is unacceptable. That must change.

This election is about remembering where we were seven and a half years ago, when President Obama came into office after eight years of Republican trickle-down economics.

The Republicans want us to forget that as a result of the greed, recklessness, and illegal behavior on Wall Street, our economy was in the worst economic downturn since the Great Depression. Some 800,000 people a month were losing their jobs. We were running up a record-breaking deficit of $1.4 trillion, and the world's financial system was on the verge of collapse.

We have come a long way in the last seven and a half years, and I thank President Obama and Vice President Biden for their leadership in pulling us out of that terrible recession.

Yes, we have made progress, but I think we can all agree that much, much more needs to be done.

This election is about which candidate understands the real problems facing this country and has offered real solutions—not just bombast, fearmongering, name-calling, and divisiveness.

We need leadership in this country which will improve the lives of working families, the children, the elderly, the sick, and the poor. We need leadership which brings our people together and makes us stronger—not leadership which insults Latinos, Muslims, women, African Americans, and veterans and divides us up.

By these measures, any objective observer will conclude that—based on her ideas and her leadership—Hillary Clinton must become the next president of the United States. The choice is not even close.

This election is about a single mom I saw in Nevada, who, with tears in her eyes, told me that she was scared to death about the future because she and her young daughter were not making it on the $10.45 an hour she was earning. This election is about that woman and the millions of other workers in this country who are struggling to survive on totally inadequate wages.

Hillary Clinton understands that if someone in America works forty hours a week, that person should not be living in poverty. She understands that we must raise the minimum wage to a living wage. And she is determined to create millions of new jobs by rebuilding our crumbling infrastructure—our roads, bridges, water systems, and wastewater plants.

But her opponent—Donald Trump—well, he has a very

different view. He does not support raising the federal minimum wage of $7.25 an hour—a starvation wage. While Donald Trump believes in huge tax breaks for billionaires, he believes that states should actually have the right to lower the minimum wage below $7.25. What an outrage!

This election is about overturning *Citizens United*, one of the worst Supreme Court decisions in the history of our country. That decision allows the wealthiest people in America, like the billionaire Koch brothers, to spend hundreds of millions of dollars buying elections and, in the process, undermine American democracy.

Hillary Clinton will nominate justices to the Supreme Court who are prepared to overturn *Citizens United* and end the movement toward oligarchy in this country. Her Supreme Court appointments will also defend a woman's right to choose, workers' rights, the rights of the LGBT community, the needs of minorities and immigrants, and the government's ability to protect the environment.

If you don't believe this election is important, if you think you can sit it out, take a moment to think about the Supreme Court justices that Donald Trump would nominate and what that would mean to civil liberties, equal rights, and the future of our country.

This election is about the thousands of young people I have met who have left college deeply in debt, and the many others who cannot afford to go to college. During the primary campaign, Secretary Clinton and I both focused on this issue, but with different approaches. Recently, however, we have come together on a proposal that will revolutionize higher education in America. It will guarantee that the children of any family in this country with an annual income of $125,000 a year or less—83 percent of our population—will be able to go to a public college or university tuition-free. That proposal also substantially reduces student debt.

This election is about climate change, the greatest environmental crisis facing our planet, and the need to leave this world in a way that is healthy and habitable for our kids and future generations. Hillary Clinton is listening to the scientists who tell us that—unless we act boldly and transform our energy system in the very near future—there will be more drought, more floods, more acidification of the oceans, more rising sea levels. She understands that when we do that, we can create hundreds of thousands of well-paying jobs.

Donald Trump? Well, like most Republicans, he chooses to reject science. He believes that climate change is a "hoax"—no need to address it. Hillary Clinton understands that a president's job is to worry about future generations, not the short-term profits of the fossil fuel industry.

This campaign is about moving the United States toward universal health care and reducing the number of people who are uninsured or underinsured. Hillary Clinton wants to see that all Americans have the right to choose a public option in their health care exchange. She believes that anyone fifty-five years or older should be able to opt in to Medicare, and she wants to see millions more Americans gain access to primary health care, dental care, mental health counseling, and low-cost prescription drugs through a major expansion of community health centers.

And what is Donald Trump's position on health care? No surprise there. Same old same old Republican contempt for working families. He wants to abolish the Affordable Care Act (ACA), throw 20 million people off the health insurance they currently have, and cut Medicaid for lower-income Americans.

Hillary Clinton also understands that millions of seniors, disabled vets, and others are struggling with the outrageously high cost of prescription drugs, and the fact that Americans pay the highest prices in the world for their medicine. She knows that Medicare must negotiate drug prices with the pharmaceutical industry, and that drug companies should not be making billions in profits while one in five Americans are unable to afford the medicine they need. The greed of the drug companies must end.

This election is about the leadership we need to pass comprehensive immigration reform and repair a broken criminal justice system. It's about making sure that young people in this country are in good schools and at good jobs, not in jail cells. Hillary Clinton understands that we have to invest in education and jobs for our young people, not more jails or incarceration.

In these stressful times for our country, this election must be about bringing our people together, not dividing us up. While Donald Trump is busy insulting one group after another, Hillary Clinton understands that our diversity is one of our greatest strengths. Yes. We become stronger when black and white, Latino, Asian American, Native American— all of us—stand together. Yes. We become stronger when men and women, young and old, gay and straight, native-born and immigrant fight to create the kind of country we all know we can become.

It is no secret that Hillary Clinton and I disagree on a number of issues. That's what this campaign has been about. That's what democracy is about. But I am happy to tell you that at the Democratic Platform Committee there was a significant coming together between the two campaigns and we produced, by far, the most progressive platform in the history of the Democratic Party. Among many other strong provisions, the Democratic Party now calls for breaking up the major financial institutions on Wall Street and the passage of a twenty-first-century Glass-Steagall Act. It also calls for strong opposition to job-killing free trade agreements like the Trans-Pacific Partnership.

Our job now is to see that platform implemented by a Democratic Senate, a Democratic House, and a Hillary Clinton presidency—and I am going to do everything I can to make that happen.

I have known Hillary Clinton for twenty-five years. I remember her as a great First Lady who broke precedent in terms of the role that a First Lady was supposed to play as she helped lead the fight for universal health care. I served with her in the United States Senate and know her as a fierce advocate for the rights of children.

Hillary Clinton will make an outstanding president and I am proud to stand with her here tonight.

OUR REVOLUTION IS FORMALLY LAUNCHED

In a nation in which our economy, our political life, and the media are largely controlled by a handful of billionaires and large corporations, the great challenge we face is how can we revitalize American democracy and create a government that represents all the people, not just the few? How do we bring millions of new people into the political process and raise political consciousness? How do we get people to recognize that democracy is not a spectator sport but a process that requires all of us, regardless of income or social status, to participate?

It is no great secret that many millions of people in our county are demoralized by our politics today and have given up on American-style democracy. They watch billionaires pour endless amounts of money into ugly TV ads and see these very same people end up with huge tax breaks. They see the rich get much richer, while politicians and the media ignore the collapse of the American middle class and the painful realities facing the poor and working families of our country.

Ordinary Americans, increasingly, are not engaged in discussions surrounding important issues. They don't vote, and they don't know or care who their local, state, or federal officials are. They don't believe that politics or government has any bearing on their lives. Democrat or Republican, progressive or conservative—who cares?

Election after election, the United States has one of the lowest voter turnouts of any major democracy on earth. In 2014, when the Republican Party won landslide victories all across the country, almost two-thirds of the American people didn't vote—the lowest turnout in seventy years. Voter turnout is especially low among lower-income Americans, whose lives are often the most greatly affected by governmental policy. It is also low among those under thirty years of age, the generation who will have to live with the decisions that are being made without their input. In America today, the state of our democracy is such that politics is something that "other" people engage in, not the average American.

I believe that the Democratic Party bears an enormous amount of responsibility for this sad state of affairs. Over the years, the party has closed its doors to ordinary Americans—working people, young people, minorities, and the poor, who once filled its ranks. As Democratic leadership became more dependent on corporate interests, it drifted further away from the hopes, needs, and participation of ordinary Americans. It became a top-down party, far removed from those struggling in our inner cities and rural counties.

Instead of holding town hall meetings with ordinary Americans, too many Democrats spend the bulk of their time raising money from the wealthy or corporate PACs. While listening to the problems of the billionaires and CEOs of large corporations, they ignore the needs of the unemployed, the underemployed, low-wage workers, and people who can't afford health care or prescription drugs.

During the course of my presidential campaign, I noticed a remarkable phenomenon. As I traveled the country, there were two political worlds that I kept interacting with. On the one hand, at the large rallies that our campaign held, many thousands of young people and working people made it clear that they wanted real change in our country. They were unafraid to stand up to the political and economic establishment and wanted to be involved in the process. For many of them, this was the first political event they had ever attended. The energy level at these rallies was extraordinarily high.

On the other hand, at the much smaller state Democratic Party functions that I attended, there were mostly older, upper-middle-class people who were party leaders, professionals, businesspeople, and campaign contributors. They had often been involved in Democratic Party politics for years, volunteering time and energy to help better the country. But, they were, as you might expect, not totally uncomfortable with the status quo. To say the least, these gatherings, which were often fund-raisers, typically generated very little excitement.

At the end of the campaign, my supporters and I faced a very simple decision. Do we, as most losing campaigns do, simply pack our bags and go home? Or do we undertake the enormously difficult task of building upon what we have accomplished during the campaign and forge a powerful progressive political movement?

We had the names and email addresses of many millions of supporters in every state in the country, and over 2 million individuals who had made campaign contributions averaging $27 apiece. State by state, we had strong leadership teams, including the almost 2,000 people who were our delegates at the Democratic National Convention in Philadelphia. We had close working relationships with some of the most progressive unions in the country, which had supported my candidacy, and with many progressive grassroots and online organizations.

On June 12, Jane and I invited some of our closest political supporters, people who had worked their hearts out on the campaign, to our home in Burlington, Vermont. These were some of the leading progressives in America, people who had been fighting for economic, social, racial, and environmental justice for their entire lives. The simple question to be discussed was: Where do we go from here? How do we build upon the successes of our campaign?

While some of our surrogates were unable to attend, the turnout was great. Among those who were there were U.S. Senator Jeff Merkley; Representatives Tulsi Gabbard, Raúl Grijalva, Peter Welch, and Keith Ellison; actress-activist Shailene Woodley; Ben Jealous, former president of the National Association for the Advancement of Colored People (NAACP); South Carolina state legislators Justin Bamberg and Terry Alexander; Cook County Illinois executive Chuy García; Larry Cohen, the former president of Communications Workers of America (CWA); Vermont political leader Rich Cassidy; author and Texas political activist Jim Hightower; environmentalist Bill McKibben; former Ohio state senator Nina Turner; National Nurses United union leader Rose-Ann DeMoro; MoveOn.org president Ilya Sheyman; Democracy for America president Jim Dean; my longtime friends and activists Ben Cohen and Jerry Greenfield; my campaign manager, Jeff Weaver; and campaign staffers Michael Briggs, Phil Fiermonte, and Shannon Jackson.

After a wide-ranging discussion, the virtually unanimous conclusion of the participants at the meeting was that it would be absurd to shut down our operations. We had accomplished too much. We had to go forward. Our goals: continue the fight for progressive legislation and ideas that would improve life for the working families of our country, work to open up the political process for millions of Americans who were now marginalized from our democracy, bring fundamental reforms to the Democratic Party, and elect progressive candidates at the federal, state, and local levels.

On August 24, a new organization was formally launched, Our Revolution, which embodied those goals. While, as an elected official, I am not legally allowed to be involved in the day-to-day activities of Our Revolution, I have watched closely from the sidelines—and have been deeply impressed by all that this organization is doing. Jeff Weaver, who was the campaign manager for my presidential campaign, took over the leadership of Our Revolution and pushed hard to hit the ground running. Former CWA president Larry Cohen, another old friend, became chair of the board.

In 2016, its first year in operation, Our Revolution played an important role in electing some of the most progressive new members of Congress, including Pramila Jayapal, of Washington State; Jamie Raskin, of Maryland; and Nanette Diaz Barragán, of California. Our Revolution helped elect new and progressive African American mayors Randall Woodfin, in Birmingham, Alabama, and Chokwe Antar Lumumba, in Jackson, Mississippi. Criminal justice reform is a major issue for Our Revolution, and they played an important role in the victory of Philadelphia district attorney Larry Krasner, who is now rewriting criminal justice law in that city.

In 2017, Nina Turner, one of my strongest surrogates in the 2016 campaign, replaced Jeff as president of the organization and continued the push for more grassroots activism. Incredibly, after only two years in existence, there are now some six hundred local chapters of Our Revolution, in almost every state in the country. Some of these chapters are large, well organized, and high-functioning. Others are smaller, with only a few members, and are struggling. But, at the end of the day, Our Revolution has managed to bring many tens of thousands of Americans into grassroots political activity, most for the first time. That is a hell of an accomplishment, and there is no political work that is more important.

During the last year, the corporate media has often pointed out that not every candidate endorsed by Our Revolution or me personally (and they are not always the same) has won his or her election. No kidding! Sadly, there were some great candidates that I, and Our Revolution separately, strongly supported who lost. But there have also been many, many great victories at every level of government.

In 2018, with very strong support from all of us, former NAACP president Ben Jealous, a founding member of Our Revolution, took on the entire Maryland Democratic political establishment in the primary, pulling off a major upset and becoming the party's nominee for governor. In the Bronx, New York, with the help of Our Revolution, Alexandria Ocasio-Cortez pulled off an even bigger upset in defeating longtime incumbent congressman and Democratic leader Joe Crowley to win the Democratic nomination in her district.

As important as winning races for Congress and governor is, there is something even more important when we look out into the future. And that is getting people involved in the political process at the local level. To that end, candidates backed by Our Revolution won races for school board, city council, mayor, county council, state legislature, and other local positions. They won in Houston,

Texas; Albuquerque, New Mexico; San Mateo, California; Wallingford, Connecticut; Clarkston, Georgia; and cities and towns all across America. They swept city council races in Cambridge and Somerville, Massachusetts. Young people, working people, are beginning to run for office all across the country, and oftentimes they are winning.

As Nina Turner states, "One of the pillars of the transformative work of Our Revolution is to clear the path to elected office for progressive candidates, who are sometimes nontraditional candidates in that they are more diverse, often first- or second-time candidates, and often overlooked by the traditional Democratic establishment. For instance, Alexandria Ocasio-Cortez was a breakout candidate who broke the party's rules, but scored in the minds of primary voters. Like so many of our other endorsed candidates, she chose to embrace progressive values rather than play it safe. Her victory and the success of many of our other endorsed candidates shows us that when we double down on progressive issues, pound the pavement like our life depends on it, we can win change for the people."

One of the important tasks that Our Revolution accomplishes is that it gives our young people, the next generation, the confidence that they can successfully run for office, and the skills they will need in order to win. An essential part of the political revolution is breaking down the barriers, psychological and financial, that intimidate potential candidates and working-class people and prevent them from getting involved in campaigns.

Many people think they can't participate in politics because they "don't know enough." They come from a working-class family and don't have a PhD in economics, education, or health care. In my view, while knowledge about public policy is important, what is far more important is honesty, a willingness to work hard and to learn. If one's heart is in the right place, if one has compassion and a sense of solidarity and justice, if one has the courage to stand up to greed and privilege, the other stuff will fall into place. In progressive politics, no one has to stand alone. We're in this together.

September 5, 2016

ON THE CAMPAIGN TRAIL
FOR CLINTON

In terms of helping Hillary Clinton win, and bringing unity to the party for the 2016 election, I was all in. I didn't need much encouragement to tell Clinton that I intended to do everything I could to help her become the next president of the United States. While on the campaign trail, I would also do what I could to help Democratic Senate candidates.

Given the nature of our Electoral College and contemporary American politics, the 2016 presidential election came down to the fifteen or twenty "battleground states" that both sides had a chance to win. That is where, of course, she focused her attention, and where I was asked to go.

Working with my staff, the Clinton campaign did a very good job making all the complicated arrangements that a campaign swing requires. Venues had to be secured, advance teams mobilized, travel and hotel arrangements made, social media mobilized to draw decent-size crowds, media notified, security arranged, and so forth. It's harder to put on a series of campaign rallies than you may think.

Throughout September, October, and November 2016, I held thirty-nine rallies in thirteen states on behalf of Hillary Clinton's campaign. In September, I was in Lebanon, New Hampshire; Kent, Ohio; and Akron, Ohio.

In October, I was in Minneapolis and Duluth, Minnesota; Des Moines, Iowa; Madison and Green Bay, Wisconsin; four cities in Michigan: Dearborn, Ann Arbor, Lansing, and Grand Rapids; Keene and Nashua, New Hampshire; Bangor, Maine; Scranton and Philadelphia, Pennsylvania; Denver and Fort Collins, Colorado; Flagstaff and Tucson, Arizona; and Reno, Nevada.

In November, I was in Plymouth and Hanover, New Hampshire; Portland, Maine; Kalamazoo and Traverse City, Michigan; Milwaukee, Wisconsin; Youngstown and Cincinnati, Ohio; Raleigh, North Carolina; Davenport, Iowa City, Ames, and Cedar Falls, Iowa; Omaha, Nebraska; Colorado Springs, Colorado; Phoenix, Arizona; and Las Vegas, Nevada.

While the turnouts for a surrogate were obviously not as large as the rallies I held for my own campaign, I ended up speaking to tens of thousands of people across the country, helped increase voter turnout, and generated a whole lot of positive media for Clinton.

One of my main goals as a surrogate was to deal up front with the issue of "personality." I was more than aware that, in various parts of the country, Clinton was not very popular. I wanted, however, to get beyond that, and to get voters to actually pay attention to what she was saying—hard to do, given much of the media's preoccupation with political gossip. This, to me, was not a campaign between Clinton's emails and allegations against the Clinton Foundation versus Trump's outrageous sexist behavior and his pathological lying. This was a campaign about very different visions for the future of the country, and I tried to make that as clear as I could.

On October 4, in Minneapolis, I said, "I speak only for myself. I get a little bit tired of hearing about personality, and 'We don't like Hillary. We don't like Trump.' Let's focus on the real issues facing the American people."

When asked, at that same event, about whether or not I was "selling out" by supporting Clinton, I stated, "I'm sure the overwhelming majority of people understand that it is absolutely imperative we do everything we can to defeat Donald Trump. I'm sure there's some people who will disagree with me. That's politics, that's democracy. I respect that. But I would also hope that people think hard about what America will look like if Donald Trump is elected."

On October 18, I was in Tucson, Arizona, for a rally attended by some 5,000 people. I focused there on some of the concrete policies that Clinton was espousing that would bring real, positive change to the lives of young people, such as eliminating tuition at public colleges for families earning less than $125,000 annually.

Amy Davidson Sorkin, a writer for *The New Yorker*, covered a rally that I did with Secretary Clinton on November 3, in Raleigh, North Carolina. She pretty much captured my attitude toward the election, writing, "One of the many things that makes Donald Trump angry is that Bernie Sanders does not seem to hold grudges. . . . 'Now, Bernie Sanders should be angry, right? Shouldn't he be angry?' Trump asked a crowd in Florida. He sounded a little bit puzzled—he would be *so* mad."

Sorkin rightfully noted, "The truth is that Bernie Sanders is very, very angry—at Donald Trump. He is angry enough to have spent weeks travelling on behalf of Hillary Clinton, speaking for her in union halls and arenas, to students and activists."

At that rally, I stated, "This campaign is not a personality contest. We're not voting for high school president. We're voting for the most powerful leader in the entire world."

Sorkin noted, "Statements like that serve to remind Sanders's supporters that they don't need to be charmed by Hillary Clinton—he is over it, and they ought to be, too. But, if personality doesn't matter, the person does."

I can't tell you that doing three or four campaign events a day is always fun, but I can tell you that, without exception, I am always moved and inspired by the people who come out to these rallies. I am deeply impressed by their love of country and their fervent desire to see us do better.

TAKING ON THE GREED OF THE PHARMACEUTICAL INDUSTRY

Virtually every single day, my office hears from constituents in Vermont and people all over this country who are sick and tired of being ripped off by the pharmaceutical industry—an industry that charges Americans, by far, the highest prices in the world for prescription drugs.

Today, there are Americans who are struggling with cancer, diabetes, heart disease, and other life-threatening illnesses who are either unable to afford the medicine they need to stay alive or are forced to go deeply into debt to buy those drugs. Each and every year, senior citizens throughout the country cut their pills in half to stretch one month's prescription into two. That is not what should be taking place in a civilized democracy.

Tragically, in our country, one out of five patients who get a prescription from their doctor is unable to fill that prescription. How insane is that? People walk into a doctor's office because they are sick, but because of the greed of the pharmaceutical industry, they are unable to afford the medicine they desperately need. How many of those patients die each year nobody knows, but I would be very surprised if we're not talking about thousands of Americans. Furthermore, as prescription drug prices soar, the overall cost of health insurance increases in our country—affecting every American.

The reason we pay two times, five times, ten times more for medicine than other countries do is pretty simple. No other country on earth allows drug companies to charge any price they want for any reason. Somebody in Burlington, Vermont, can walk into a pharmacy and find that the price they pay for the medicine they've been using for years has doubled or tripled. And in the United States, that is perfectly legal. Drug companies can and do raise prices, sometimes in outrageous ways, simply because they can, because the market will bear it.

The former CEO of Gilead, John Martin, became a billionaire because his drug company charged $1,000 a pill for Sovaldi, a hepatitis C drug that costs a mere $1 to manufacture and can be bought in India for just $4.

Meanwhile, with Americans dying because they cannot afford the medications they need, the profits of the pharmaceutical industry soar. In 2015, five of the biggest drug companies made a total of over $50 billion in profits, while the top ten pharmaceutical industry CEOs made $327 million in total compensation.

Why do we pay the highest prices in the world for prescription drugs when millions of Americans cannot afford the medicine they desperately need? Why can drug companies raise their prices at any time, for any reason? Why, year after year, is the pharmaceutical industry one of the most profitable sectors in the United States? Why do CEOs of drug companies receive huge compensation packages?

The answer to these questions is simple. The pharmaceutical

industry is one of the wealthiest and most powerful political forces in this country. Over the past twenty years, the industry has spent more than $4 billion on lobbying and campaign contributions to get Congress and state legislatures to do its bidding. They have more than 1,200 lobbyists in Washington, DC, alone, including many former political leaders. They own the Republican Party and have significant influence over the Democratic Party as well.

Here is a recent example of the power of the pharmaceutical industry and the unlimited amounts of money they have to protect their interests. In 2016, a group of consumer activists, led by the National Nurses United union, secured enough signatures to put an initiative on the California ballot, with the goal of lowering drug prices.

Specifically, this proposal would require California to pay no more than the Department of Veterans Affairs (VA) does for prescription drugs. Because the VA is the only federal agency that is required by law to negotiate with the drug companies, it pays lower prices for prescription drugs than any other agency in America. In fact, the VA pays about 24 percent less for drugs than most government agencies and about 40 percent less than Medicare Part D.

Proposition 61, the California Drug Price Relief Act, as the initiative was called, was a win-win. It would have saved the taxpayers of California about $1 billion a year, and it would have lowered the price of prescription drugs for millions of people in the state who were on Medicaid.

As someone who has been a leader in Congress for decades in opposition to the greed of the drug companies, I was more than happy to support this grassroots effort. If we could pass an initiative to lower drug prices in California, our largest state, there was no question in my mind that this effort would spread all across the country. As part of my support for this initiative, I filmed an ad and published op-eds in the *Los Angeles Times* and other papers. I also went to several well-attended rallies around the state on October 17, encouraging voters in California to approve the initiative.

Here is what is so extraordinary and telling about the process surrounding the California initiative, and speaks to the corruption of the American political process. Despite the fact that California is regarded as one of the most liberal states in the country, not one statewide Democratic leader was prepared to stand up and take on the drug companies. Further, there was almost no support from the large Democratic congressional delegation. There was also minimal support from the strong Democratic majority in the state legislature. Needless to say, there was absolutely no support for the initiative from Republicans. In other words, when it came to taking on the pharmaceutical industry, the political class virtually disappeared.

In order to defeat Proposition 61, the prescription drug industry showed us what political power was all about. They also showed us the endless supply of money they have to protect their interests over the needs of the American people.

Unbelievably, in one state and on one ballot initiative, they spent $131 million to make sure Proposition 61 failed. Let me repeat that. The drug companies spent $131 million to defeat one ballot initiative that would have lowered drug prices in one state.

In the end, despite all of the money, the lies and the distortions the drug companies spread, and the refusal of political leaders to take a stand, Proposition 61 still received 46 percent of the vote on Election Day.

When I talk about a rigged economic system that benefits the rich, and a corrupt political system that benefits the powerful, the campaign to defeat Proposition 61 in California tells you everything you need to know.

ELECTION NIGHT

Election night. I was tired. I had just returned to Burlington after a final campaign stop in Las Vegas. During the last week alone, I had done seventeen events for Clinton in eleven states, from Maine to Nevada.

This was the most important election of our lifetime. All of us had to come together to defeat Trump. And I had done my best.

On the plane back from Las Vegas, the discussion obviously centered on who would win the presidential election and which party would control the Senate. My political gut gave Clinton a 3–1 chance of winning. In other words, I thought she was going to win, but I was not going to be shocked if she didn't. In talking to Jane when I got back, it turned out that she was not quite so confident. She sensed that some people who were going to be voting for Trump were not necessarily telling the pollsters that. She thought that Trump would likely win.

My concerns about the outcome of the election centered on the growing enthusiasm that Trump seemed to be generating. I kept thinking about an outdoor rally I had done with Clinton a few days earlier, on November 3, in Raleigh, North Carolina. It was a beautiful evening, and the venue was great. The crowd was large, diverse, and full of energy, and I felt very good about the event. My excitement was tempered, however, when I later learned that Trump did a rally on a farm not far away, with a much larger turnout.

Election night for a political family like mine is something of a ritual. We kind of do the same thing every two years. We did it when I won my congressional elections, we did it when I won my Senate races, and we do it for presidential elections. Rather than being with a large crowd in some hotel ballroom, unable to focus on the returns, Jane and I typically have a small group of family and friends over to the house to watch the results come in and make sense of what's happening.

Election night after election night, the kids and old friends Richard and Linda Sugarman and Huck and Buff Gutman come over to the house. We sit around the TV and a computer or two and, like most Americans, watch the returns come in. Nothing fancy. We munch on cold cuts, cookies, and potato chips and have some wine and beer.

The usual custom is that when the results become apparent, Jane and I would head downtown to a hotel ballroom to be part of the Vermont Democratic Party gathering. Even though I was not on the ballot that night, I expected to congratulate local candidates who had won, including a good friend who had just been elected lieutenant governor. I would also say a few words to the crowd and do some media interviews. That's what I expected to do.

On the night of November 8, we never made it downtown. We were just too depressed. Donald Trump had been elected president of the United States.

Needless to say, in the following weeks and months, half the country obsessed over how Trump had won. I was one of those people. How could someone who had run a hateful, racist, xenophobic campaign be elected president of the United States? How could someone who was seen on video boasting about his assaults on women be elected president of the United States? How could someone who had been involved in more than 3,000 lawsuits in his business career be elected president of the United States? How could someone who lied over and over again in the most shameful manner be elected president of the United States? How could someone who had little interest in or knowledge of public policy be elected president of the United States?

In the following years, I would spend a great deal of time trying to answer those questions and, more important, making sure that a tragedy of this magnitude never happens again.

PART OF THE DEMOCRATIC SENATE LEADERSHIP

Following the election, Chuck Schumer, Democratic Senate leader, asked me to be part of the ten-member Senate Democratic Leadership team. In that capacity, I serve with, in addition to Schumer, Dick Durbin, of Illinois; Patty Murray, of Washington; Debbie Stabenow, of Michigan; Elizabeth Warren, of Massachusetts; Amy Klobuchar, of Minnesota; Mark Warner, of Virginia; Joe Manchin, of West Virginia; and Tammy Baldwin, of Wisconsin. My official position is chairman of outreach.

To be honest, I was initially ambivalent about taking on the position. There are only twenty-four hours in a day, and a strong part of me wanted to devote my time to fighting for the progressive legislation that I would be introducing, consistent with my presidential campaign—raising the minimum wage to $15 an hour, Medicare for All, making public colleges and universities tuition-free, ending corporate welfare, rebuilding our crumbling infrastructure, and so forth. I also wanted to pay strong attention to the needs of my own state of Vermont. That's a lot to do.

Further, I must confess that I am not a great fan of the interminable inside-the-Beltway meetings that would clearly be part of the job. There are leadership meetings on Monday afternoon and Tuesday morning, in addition to the general Democratic Caucus lunch meetings on Tuesday and Thursday. That's a lot of meetings.

On the other hand, it is no small thing to be part of leadership and help shape the priorities and strategies of the Democratic Caucus. During the presidential campaign, I received more than 13 million votes, and it was more than appropriate that those supporters, and the policies they believe in, had a strong voice at the highest level of the Democratic Party. In addition, being chairman of outreach would give me additional resources as we traveled the country rallying the American people around a progressive agenda.

After a lot of discussion with Jane, my staff, and my political advisers, I concluded that the pluses of being part of leadership far outweighed the minuses, and I asked Chuck to put me on the team. After a few days of thinking about it and talking to other senators, he concluded that it made sense for the party. My name was announced with the others at a Capitol Hill press conference.

Chuck Schumer became Democratic leader in 2017, when Harry Reid retired. Harry served as majority leader when Democrats controlled the Senate. He and I were friends and had a good working relationship. Harry was far more progressive than most people knew, and he was very helpful to me on some major issues.

I have long been a champion of seeing the government create a strong primary health care system so that every American, regardless of income, can visit a doctor whenever he or she needs to. The best vehicle for doing that was a major expansion of the Federally Qualified Health Center (FQHC) program. In Vermont, almost one out of four people now gets their primary health care, dental care, and mental health counseling at a community health center. Harry and I talked often about the importance of community health centers, and how they were working effectively in Vermont as well as in his own state of Nevada.

I will never forget the day Reid called me into his office and told me that he was putting $12 billion more into the program as part of the Affordable Care Act, the largest expansion in FQHC history. As a result, many millions more Americans have been able to access the health care they need. We also substantially increased funding for the National Health Service Corps, which provides debt forgiveness and scholarships for doctors, dentists, and nurses prepared to practice in medically underserved areas. Thank you, Harry.

I have known Chuck Schumer for twenty-eight years, going back to when we were both in the House of Representatives and served together on the House Banking Committee. We even grew up in the same Flatbush neighborhood in Brooklyn, and although we did not know each other as kids, we went to the same elementary school, P.S. 197, and the same high school, James Madison. Chuck and I have always looked at politics from different perspectives, but we're friends and have worked well together.

As I assumed my place in the Senate Democratic Leadership, I thought back to the strange and winding road that got me to this position, and how different my political history was compared to that of my colleagues. And it was very different. It's not just that my first visits to Washington, DC, were for antiwar and civil rights demonstrations. It's not just that I was so far removed from conventional politics that I was never inside the Capitol until after I ran for Congress. It's not that I never really knew a Democratic or a Republican Party official until I was elected mayor of Burlington. It's not just that I remain the longest-serving Independent in U.S. congressional history. It's that my political career began in a very different place than that of anyone else in Congress.

I started in electoral politics in 1971, when, as a member of a small third party called the Liberty Union, I ran for the U.S. Senate in Vermont, in a special election against a Republican and a Democrat. The Republican won easily, and I received 2 percent of the vote. That's right. No misprint here: just 2 percent of the vote. And that was pretty good. One year later, I ran for governor of Vermont and received 1 percent of the vote. In 1974, I ran for Senate again and received 4 percent of the vote, and in 1976, I ran for governor again and received 6 percent of the vote. How's that for a political success story? Not quite the well-planned path forward that most politicians take on the road to the U.S. Senate.

In 1977, I resigned from the Liberty Union Party. There were other things I had to do. Given the fact that the party had virtually no money or establishment support, I was proud of what we had accomplished over the years. Doing newspaper, radio, and television interviews, participating in debates, and handing out literature on the streets, we educated Vermonters on some of the most important issues facing the state and the country. We may not have won elections, but we did have an impact on changing political consciousness in a state that, at that point, was one of the most Republican in the country.

Members of the Liberty Union were vigorous in opposition to the Vietnam War and for a democratic foreign policy. We fought hard for economic justice and in support of unions and consumers, and strongly supported civil rights and civil liberties. We forced Republican and Democratic candidates to discuss issues they would have preferred to ignore. Further, with a number of our statewide candidates being women, we played a significant role in breaking down sexism in state politics.

After leaving the Liberty Union Party and withdrawing from electoral politics, I started a small nonprofit organization called the American People's Historical Society. Working with a few friends, I wrote, produced, and sold filmstrips on state history for schools in Vermont and other places in New England.

Producing filmstrips was actually a lot of fun, and I was making a living. I liked doing the research and writing, dabbling in photography, and narrating the audio. I also enjoyed traveling around Vermont, New Hampshire, and Massachusetts selling the filmstrips from school to school.

In 1979, with changing technology, I wrote and produced a video on the life and times of Eugene Victor Debs that was sold to colleges around the country. Debs was a great American who played an enormously important role in our history, but he was unknown to most people. He was one of the leading trade union leaders of the late nineteenth century, the founder of the American Socialist Party, and a six-time candidate for president of the United States. In 1920, he received nearly 1 million votes for president while he was in jail for his opposition to World War I. Many of the ideas that Debs campaigned on were later adopted by FDR and incorporated into the New Deal. Today, I have a plaque of Debs on a wall in my Senate office.

In 1981, after I had taken a five-year break from electoral politics, a group of friends suggested that I run for mayor of Burlington, the city where I lived, as an Independent. I would be running against a five-term Democratic incumbent who had the support of the entire business and political establishment. We had no money, no organizational support, and very little name recognition. Nobody gave us a chance—and I mean nobody. But as the campaign progressed, we began putting together a diverse grassroots coalition—trade unions, low-income groups, women, environmentalists, neighborhood activists. On bitter-cold days in January and February, volunteers and I knocked on thousands of doors.

And, to everybody's shock, we won. A late endorsement by the Burlington Patrolman's Association, considered to be a conservative group, probably put us over the top. On election night, the margin of our victory was 14 votes. After the recount, it was 10 votes. It was one of the great political upsets in Vermont history and a victory that the state's largest newspaper later referred to as "the story of the decade."

In Burlington then, we had two-year mayoral terms, and I won reelection in 1983 and 1985 by defeating a Democrat and a Republican in each contest. In 1983, we almost doubled voter turnout over the 1979 election as we won landslide victories in the low-income and working-class wards of the city. In 1987, the two parties actually combined around one candidate, but we won that election as well, with 54 percent of the vote.

In 1986, I ran for governor of Vermont against a Democratic incumbent, Madeleine Kunin, who won reelection. I came in third place, with 14 percent of the vote. In 1988, I ran for an open seat in the U.S. Congress. While I lost that election, I came in second place, losing to the Republican by 3 points, but handily defeating the Democrat, who came in a distant third. In 1990, I defeated the incumbent Republican by 16 points and became the first Independent elected to Congress in forty years. I ended up serving in the House for sixteen years.

In 2006, Vermont's Senator Jim Jeffords retired, and I ran to replace him. My major opponent was a Republican businessman, Richie Tarrant, the wealthiest person in the state. Not only did Tarrant spend more money per vote on that election than any Senate candidate in American history, and far more than anyone in

Vermont had ever spent, but he ran the most negative campaign the state had ever seen. It was nasty! I couldn't turn on the TV without seeing myself being portrayed as some kind of enemy of humanity. It turned out, however, that Tarrant's well-paid consultants forgot to tell him that the people of Vermont didn't like negative advertising. We won that election with a vote of 65 percent to 32 percent.

In 2012, I won reelection against a Republican candidate, with 71 percent of the vote.

And now I was a member of the Senate Democratic Leadership.

SAVING THE AFFORDABLE CARE ACT

In late December 2016, I gathered my senior staff in our office conference room. It was six weeks since Donald Trump had been elected president and about a month before he would take the oath of office.

No one could know for sure what Trump's long-term agenda would be, but one thing was certain. He had campaigned vigorously against the Affordable Care Act, and the Republicans who controlled both bodies of Congress had made it crystal clear that they wanted to repeal it. We needed a plan to fight back. We could not allow 30 million Americans to lose their health insurance.

Already, Senate Republicans were gearing up to put in motion a process known as "budget reconciliation." This would allow them to repeal the ACA with just 51 votes, rather than the 60 votes that would normally be needed. For us to win, we needed to hold on to all 48 Democratic senators and pick up 3 Republicans.

My position on health care has been clear to the people of Vermont and America for a very long time. To me, health care is a human right, not a privilege. I believe our nation needs to end the international embarrassment of being the only major country on earth not to guarantee health care for all in a cost-effective way. That's why I have been a longtime supporter of a Medicare for All, single-payer program.

I voted for the Affordable Care Act because, while it did not go anywhere near as far as I wanted, it did provide health insurance for about 20 million more Americans, ended the abomination of people being denied insurance coverage because of preexisting conditions, expanded primary health care, and significantly improved health care coverage for women.

This struggle, however, was not just about protecting the ACA. It was about defending Planned Parenthood. Despite polling that showed overwhelming national support for the high-quality work that Planned Parenthood was doing, the Republicans wanted to defund that organization as part of the ACA repeal process. If they were successful, over 2 million women would lose access to their health care providers, despite the fact that no federal money was used for abortions.

As we discussed how best to go forward in defending the ACA, it became clear to my staff and me that we needed to mount an unprecedented grassroots campaign. In state after state, ordinary Americans needed to stand up and tell the Republicans what it would mean to their lives and the lives of their family members if they lost the health care they had.

Obviously my office could not do this alone. We had to coordinate efforts with progressive organizations throughout the country, and with Democratic offices in the Senate and the House. As chair of the Democratic Outreach Committee, I met with Chuck Schumer and proposed a plan for a series of rallies on January 15, less than a week before Trump was to be inaugurated. Schumer liked the idea and signed on.

We would very intentionally do the major rally in Macomb County, Michigan, a swing county that had gone for Obama in 2012 but voted strongly for Trump in 2016. I would be there, Schumer would be there, and Michigan senators Debbie Stabenow and Gary Peters would also be speaking. On the same day, we would also hold simultaneous rallies throughout the country with Democratic senators, House members, and other public officials. The word had to go out. We would not allow the ACA to be repealed without a fight. The Republicans were going to pay a very heavy political price for their disgraceful piece of legislation.

In order for us to be successful, there were several major obstacles that had to be overcome. First, time was short, and the Christmas season is not a great moment for organizing anything. People are preoccupied with the holidays. Second, the idea of doing simultaneous rallies around the country is a new and radical one for Democrats in Congress. Many Democratic senators and House members are not much into grassroots politics. This would be a whole new thing.

Nonetheless, despite the problems we faced, we succeeded in this new venture beyond our wildest expectations. Given the time and organizational constraints that we were working under, the results we achieved were remarkable. More than seventy rallies were held around the country, and most of them were very successful. The largest was in Macomb County, where over 8,000 people came to an outdoor rally on a very cold day.

In Massachusetts, Senators Elizabeth Warren and Ed Markey led a well-attended event outside Faneuil Hall in Boston. Maryland's congressional delegation held a rally at Bowie State

University. Senator Tim Kaine joined an event in Virginia, and Senator Dick Durbin hosted hundreds in Chicago. Former Maryland governor Martin O'Malley even sang with a crowd in the Utah State Capitol.

During the following week, as we spoke to senators and checked out local media reports, we were able to fully appreciate the success of the effort.

WCMH-TV described the event in Columbus, Ohio: "Hundreds of people filled a room at the UA Local 189 Plumbers and Pipefitters building, looking for a way to stop the process of repealing the Affordable Care Act. The co-organizer of the Ohio Revolution, Puja Datta, said the Our First Stand rally is about more than just health care. 'It's time for us to take politics back in our own hands,' Datta said."

The *Independent Record* in Helena, Montana, reported, "About 200 people packed the Capitol Rotunda in support of health care programs on Sunday afternoon. The Save Our Health Care rally in Helena ran alongside others in Missoula and Bozeman."

The *Capitol Gazette* in Annapolis described the Maryland event: "Hundreds of people crowded into the ballroom of the Bowie State University student center on Sunday to signal their support for the Affordable Care Act, part of a 'national day of action' that brought similar rallies to cities around the country. More people showed up to the Bowie rally than the ballroom at Bowie State could hold."

The *Washington Post*, recognizing the grassroots energy, reported on the success of the rallies around the country: "Police estimated about 600 people showed up in Portland, Maine. Hundreds also attended events in Newark, New Jersey, Johnston, Rhode Island, Richmond, Virginia and Boston."

Perhaps the best headline came from the *Guardian*: "Democrats

Turn to American People to Protect Obamacare from Looming Repeal."

January 15 was not the only day for coordinated, well-attended rallies around the country in opposition to the repeal of the Affordable Care Act. On February 25, there were another one hundred rallies. I was in Topeka, Kansas, that night with thousands of people who were doing all they could to prevent millions of their fellow Americans from losing their health care.

In New Jersey, according to NJ.com, "Over 300 people gathered in front of the Bergen County Courthouse Saturday to rally against the repeal of the Affordable Care Act. Crowds packed the steps of the courthouse to protest President Donald Trump's health care agenda which includes the repeal of the Affordable Care Act and the defunding of Planned Parenthood."

Grassroots activism against the repeal of the ACA was not limited to rallies. Republican congressmen, who would normally have fifty or seventy-five people show up at their town hall meetings, now saw hundreds of irate citizens at these meetings who were demanding an explanation for why they cast their terrible vote. In some congressional districts, more than a thousand people showed up, and they were not happy. They were fighting for their lives and the lives of their loved ones. The meetings became very personal and emotional.

According to *Washington Post* reporter Dave Weigel, "At a town hall in Chico, Calif., in the most Democratic portion of a deep-red district, Representative Doug LaMalfa (R) faced furious complaints about the repeal vote, with constituents accusing him of acting to bring about their deaths. 'I hope you suffer the same painful fate as those millions that you have voted to remove health care from,' one constituent told LaMalfa. 'May you die in pain.'"

Politico reported that in Santa Clarita, California,

*Rep. Steve Knight tried desperately to distinguish himself as
a moderate Republican and counterpoint to an unpopular
President Donald Trump during a 90-minute town hall here
in sunny Santa Clarita. But when it came to his recent vote to
repeal Obamacare, the vulnerable Californian couldn't escape
the public grilling. He was regularly mocked, jeered and
interrupted by a crowd that seemed unsatisfied with his
answers.*

*"I am angry and disappointed that you voted to repeal the
Affordable Care Act, then replace it with garbage," said one
constituent in the front-row of a high school auditorium—
the first of at least 10 health policy questions of the evening. The
crowd whooped.*

On May 4, 2017, the House of Representatives had voted,
217–213, to repeal the Affordable Care Act. Now the fight came
to the Senate.

Working with MoveOn.org, we decided to do another series of
rallies in states that Trump had won—in Pittsburgh, Pennsylvania; Charleston, West Virginia; and Columbus, Ohio. Given the
fact that no one knew when the ACA vote in the Senate might be
coming, we had to move fast. It took an enormous amount of work
on the part of my staff, led by Ari Rabin-Havt, to pull these events
together, but we did it. Some thirty-six hours after we decided to
go forward, we had venues booked, supporters on the ground, and
advance teams out in all three cities.

Given the short time that we had to prepare for these events, I
had no idea what to expect when I walked into the Pittsburgh convention center on Saturday afternoon, June 24. Needless to say, I
was very pleased when I saw that 1,600 people had come out to
fight against Republican attempts to take away their health care.

The *Post-Gazette* wrote the next day, "Vermont Sen. Bernie Sanders called some 1,600 Pittsburghers to the ramparts Saturday night, urging the crowd to oppose Republican efforts to repeal the Affordable Care Act. 'We will not be part of a process which takes from working families, takes from the sick, takes from the children, takes from the elderly, takes from the poor, in order to give huge tax breaks to people who don't need them,' he thundered in a David L. Lawrence Convention Center ballroom."

Local TV led with our rally that night, and it was on the front page of the papers in the morning. That was exactly the point. By holding these rallies, not only did we reach thousands of people directly, but our message reached hundreds of times that through the local media.

The next day, we held another great rally in Columbus, for more than 2,000 people. As the *Columbus Dispatch* reported, "The Sanders event drew a characteristically energetic audience, but it was a palpable anxiety and anger energizing the crowd. Boos and sharp cries of 'Don't take away our health care' and 'They work for us' interrupted rally speakers. Along with the plan to scale back Medicaid, speakers denounced provisions in the bill to eliminate federal dollars for Planned Parenthood. They also criticized Republican lawmakers for crafting the legislation behind closed doors and without a public hearing."

From there we headed to West Virginia, one of the poorest states in the country and a state that Trump won by 42 points. More than 1,000 people attended the event in Charleston.

We went out of our way to make certain that these rallies were not dominated by politicians, and that ordinary people got a chance to speak. At almost every rally, we had three or four local people from all walks of life who got up, told their stories, and talked about how the policies being debated in Washington, DC, had a real-world impact on their lives. During our health care tour we heard from patients and doctors, from women who needed Planned Parenthood to get health care, and from those who would be denied care because they had preexisting conditions. Charleston was no different. There I saw one of the most powerful speakers on the tour, Rusty Williams.

A West Virginia native, Rusty is a tattoo artist who was diagnosed with testicular cancer. Without insurance, he almost died. This is a man who, in the very literal sense of the word, fought for his life against a system and a bureaucracy that did not want him to receive the care he desperately needed. Rusty's passionate and brilliant speech was powerful testimony as to why health care should be a right for every man, woman, and child in the United States, not one that is available solely to those who can afford it. Rusty later recorded a video for us that was seen by millions of people.

Early on the morning of July 28, the bill to repeal the Affordable Care Act finally came to the floor of the Senate. There were forty-eight Democrats in the Senate. They all voted no. There were fifty-two Republicans. Forty-nine of them voted yes. Three Republicans—Susan Collins, of Maine; Lisa Murkowski, of Alaska; and John McCain, of Arizona—voted no.

It was a long, hard fight.

We won.

INAUGURATION DAY

As is customary, the members of the U.S. Senate assembled at 11:30 a.m. in the Senate chamber before walking out to the Capitol patio for the noon inaugural ceremony. It looked like rain. Senate staff distributed plastic ponchos. I didn't need one. I had my all-purpose, super-warm, hooded Vermont coat. It didn't look quite formal or senatorial, but it did the trick.

I walked out alongside Senator John McCain and ended up sitting between him and Senator Jim Inhofe. I was a few yards away from Trump when he was sworn in and gave his speech. Jane and other spouses sat farther behind. Hundreds of thousands of people filled the Mall in front.

My most vivid memory of that day, in addition to getting booed by the Trump crowd when my image flashed on the large TV screen, was Michelle Obama walking down the stairs to her seat at the inauguration alongside President Obama. Her attire and tone said it all. The beautiful and fashionable First Lady was clearly not at this event to celebrate. Wearing a staid outfit and a serious countenance, without saying a word, she seemed to be showing the world her discomfort and displeasure with the odious man who was replacing her husband. Hillary and Bill Clinton were also there. They didn't look too happy, either.

Trump's inaugural speech gave me my clearest sense yet as to the kind of phony and demagogue he was. Other than his racism and xenophobia, it's not clear that he really has any strong beliefs other than those that are politically expedient. As economist Bruce Bartlett once wrote about Trump, "He's been on every side of every issue from every point of view as far as I can tell."

Trump was once a significant contributor to the Democratic Party and considered himself more Democrat than Republican. Now he hates Democrats. He was once pro-choice. Now he is vehemently anti-abortion. He once actually believed in a Canadian-style single-payer health care system. Now he wants to abolish the modest Affordable Care Act. He once proposed a major tax on wealth. Now he wants to give massive tax breaks to billionaires. He once supported a ban on assault weapons. Now he is a strong ally of the National Rifle Association (NRA).

What position will he advocate tomorrow? Who knows?

What I found particularly disturbing about Trump's speech was not only his dishonesty and hypocrisy, but his clearly calculated effort to appeal to the deep-seated prejudices in our culture. Instead of trying to bring the American people together in all their diversity, as most presidents have attempted, Trump was prepared to stir up our worst fears and prejudices and turn us against each other for cheap political gain.

For hundreds of years this country has struggled with all kinds of terrible discrimination based on race, religion, gender, nationality, and sexual orientation. But as a result of the civil rights movement, the women's movement, and other grassroots efforts, we have made significant progress in breaking down those barriers—progress we should be extremely proud of. It was hard to believe that, instead of someone who would continue to move us forward into a less discriminatory society, we had a president who wanted to take us backward. How disgraceful was that!

But it was not only his divisiveness and ultra-nationalism that was offensive. I found one section of his speech almost laughable. He said:

> *For too long, a small group in our nation's capital has reaped the rewards of government while the people have borne the cost.*
>
> *Washington flourished—but the people did not share in its wealth.*
>
> *Politicians prospered—but the jobs left, and the factories closed.*
>
> *The establishment protected itself, but not the citizens of our country.*
>
> *Their victories have not been your victories; their triumphs have not been your triumphs; and while they celebrated in our nation's capital, there was little to celebrate for struggling families all across our land.*
>
> *That all changes—starting right here, and right now, because this moment is your moment: it belongs to you.*

Wonderful rhetoric, but a total lie. The truth was that the "small group" that had most benefited from America's prosperity were many of the billionaires who had supported his campaign, whom he had invited to the VIP section that day and who were now seated a few feet away from him. It was already clear that they would be the ones who would benefit most from the policies Trump wanted to implement. In fact, Trump would end up appointing more billionaires to his administration than any president in history.

Yet he had the chutzpah to tell the American people that this was *their* day.

After the speech, Jane and I attended an inaugural lunch in the Capitol with many members of Congress and assorted VIPs. The new president, his wife, Melania, and other family members and congressional leaders were seated at the front table. At the reception, Jane and I were pleased to say a few words to President Jimmy Carter and his wife, Rosalynn. We also said hello to Bill and Hillary Clinton. A very pleasant young woman introduced herself to us. It was one of Vice President Pence's daughters. Among others at our table was General John Kelly, Trump's nominee for secretary of Homeland Security.

As I left the Capitol that day, I was angry. The country faced enormous problems that the American people wanted to see resolved. And I wanted to begin work on them. But under Trump and Republican leadership, I knew there was no way that would happen. Instead, we would have to spend at least the next two years in a defensive mode, preventing bad situations from becoming worse.

Instead of providing health care to all, we would have to prevent the dismantling of the Affordable Care Act. Instead of addressing the obscene level of income and wealth inequality in our country, we would have to prevent massive tax breaks for the rich and cuts to vitally important programs for working people. Instead of addressing the planetary crisis of climate change, we would have to prevent the dismantling of the Environmental Protection Agency. Instead of moving to overturn the disastrous *Citizens United* Supreme Court decision, we would have to fight outrageous efforts at voter suppression. And on and on.

Needless to say, on the day of the inauguration and afterward, my thoughts turned to determining how we could most effectively resist Trump and his reactionary agenda. How could we create a grassroots movement that would be prepared to stand up and fight back?

Well, I didn't have long to wait to see how the American people were prepared to respond.

On the night of the inauguration, Jane and I flew back to Vermont. The next afternoon, we were in a car driving thirty-seven miles east to Montpelier, Vermont, the state capital, to attend the Women's March. Over the years, I had made that drive, from Burlington to Montpelier, a million times. But this trip was different. On an interstate where there was usually very little traffic, our car was stuck in a traffic jam the likes of which I had never seen on a Vermont interstate highway. It appeared that half the state was heading to Montpelier for the Women's March.

Montpelier is a small city of a little more than 7,500 people. Incredibly, more people traveled into Montpelier for that rally than actually lived in the city. The media later estimated the crowd to be about 15,000, one of the largest rallies ever held in our small state. In fact, the crowd was so large that the police had to shut down the off-ramp from the interstate into the city because there was just no more parking. With a police escort, we managed to get to the State House just in time for my remarks.

In the evening, we learned that the Women's March in Washington was attended by some 500,000 people. Trump wasn't happy with it, but that rally attracted more people than his inaugural speech. But, of course, it wasn't just Washington. Millions of people took to the streets all across the nation and, in fact, all over the world. Amazingly, what happened in Montpelier was happening everywhere. I was very proud that some of the lead organizers of the Women's March, including Linda Sarsour, had been active in my campaign. What an unbelievable job they did!

By bringing millions of people together to fight back against Donald Trump and his policies, the Women's March launched a new grassroots movement, not only for women but for all of us. It was the grassroots energy of the Women's March that fueled much of the energy we have seen over the past two years—an energy whose intensity has only increased, not diminished. When I got home that evening, inspired by the Montpelier rally and all that I had seen during that day, I sent out a tweet that read, "President Trump, you made a big mistake. By trying to divide us up by race, religion, gender and nationality you actually brought us closer." It turned out to be the most successful tweet sent by any member of Congress during the year. It received 970,801 likes, 452,079 retweets, and 13,814 replies.

The resistance had begun, and I intended to do all I could to be a part of it.

A NEW WAY TO COMMUNICATE

When we talk about the political revolution, we are not only talking about a progressive agenda and a grassroots political movement. We are talking about the necessity of finding a new way to communicate with the American people.

Unlike Trump, I do not believe that mainstream media is "fake news" or an "enemy of the people." I don't believe that most reporters carry a grudge and intentionally try to destroy politicians. I do believe, however, as I have said many times, that for a variety of obvious reasons, multinational conglomerates that own our media are not interested in analyzing the power of big-money interests, or the needs of working families.

A month after his inauguration, Donald Trump came to Capitol Hill to deliver his first speech to a joint session of Congress. As I have done throughout my congressional career, I was in attendance in the House chamber for the president's speech, as were virtually all members of Congress.

The president's prime-time speech is always carried by all of the major networks, which customarily also cover the response from the opposition party. The Democratic Party chose Steve Beshear, former governor of Kentucky, to make that speech. Beshear was a strong supporter of the Affordable Care Act and had transformed health care in his state by greatly expanding the Medicaid program under that law.

The Democrats, correctly, wanted to show a contrast between Trump's desire to repeal the Affordable Care Act, and throw millions off the health care they had, and a state like Kentucky, where the ACA was wildly successful and popular.

While I did not want to step on the official Democratic response, I knew that the nature of my opposition would be different from that offered by Governor Beshear, a moderate Democrat. I would be speaking not only against the repeal of the Affordable Care Act, but also for an agenda that represented the needs of working families and was prepared to take on the powerful elites in our country.

Following a presidential address to Congress, most members respond by speaking through the mainstream media. Journalists from newspapers, television, and radio fill up Statuary Hall, outside the House chamber. It is extraordinarily chaotic as members of Congress leave the House floor and fight for position to speak in front of TV cameras, radio microphones, and print reporters.

Given the unprecedented times we were living in, I thought it was important to respond in an unprecedented way. Why not use new technology and speak directly to the American people?

A week before the speech, my staff and I explored the idea of using the Democratic Caucus's television studio for a livestream speech via social media. This studio is a full-fledged broadcast facility, and the quality of their work is excellent. I was confident they could do a good job.

Our challenge was not only determining the best way to respond but also figuring out exactly what to say. Writing a critique of a speech that you can roughly anticipate but which has not yet been given is not easy. It requires a great deal of nimbleness. We began drafting my remarks on the morning of the president's speech based on media reports of what would be in it. As the president was speaking, and as I listened attentively on the House floor, my staff kept track of what was being said and altered the draft to make sure we were responding exactly to his remarks and not missing any important points.

My staff did a great job, but I like to write my own speeches. Therefore, the speech would not be ready to go until I worked to make sure it was precisely what I wanted to say. So, following Trump's address, I raced off the House floor and back to my office in the Senate to put together the final draft. We didn't have a lot of time. Beshear was already speaking. When the speech was finally completed, it was emailed upstairs and put into the studio's teleprompter.

It was now about 11:00 p.m. Eastern Standard Time. The president had spoken, and Governor Beshear had given the official Democratic response. Would anybody still be awake? Would there be an audience for my speech?

Delivering a speech in a closed studio is not easy. It is very different from speaking at a rally, where you absorb the energy of the people, feed off their responses, and develop a rhythm that works. At a public event, you can see, hear, and feel how people are reacting and make the necessary course corrections. In an antiseptic studio, where you are alone and simply looking into a TV camera, you do your best, but you have no idea how people are responding.

In my speech, I wanted to highlight not only what Trump had

said but, equally important, what he hadn't said. I wanted to contrast the views he had expressed as a candidate with what he was actually proposing as president.

Interestingly, after running a campaign promising the American people that he wouldn't cut Social Security or Medicare, he didn't mention those programs once. After a campaign in which he told us he was going to take on Wall Street and drain the swamp of special interests, he neglected to mention that he had appointed more billionaires to his administration than any previous president. After a campaign in which he promised to stand up for working people and take on the establishment, he didn't once mention the words "income and wealth inequality."

Needless to say, he did not address such major national crises as climate change, *Citizens United* and voter suppression, our broken criminal justice system, or the need for comprehensive immigration reform.

Jane was with me in DC that night, and as I walked out of the recording studio, she kissed me, and that was all I needed to know. My office staff and the staff of the media center looked elated.

"So, did anybody watch?" I asked.

It turned out they had. More than 8.5 million people ended up watching that speech on Facebook alone. It was a HUGE success.

Ultimately, more important than the content of my speech was the fact that we had demonstrated a new way that we could speak directly to millions of people. Further, we discovered that not only did people in the United States watch that speech, but it was viewed all over the world.

With a greater understanding of what the internet revolution was all about and the power of social media, we now had the opportunity to do something other public officials had never done. We could communicate directly to millions of viewers on our own terms. Given that the progressive perspective is very rarely presented by the corporate media, this, for us, was especially important.

As a result of the success of that evening, we have since made social media central to the efforts of our office. Virtually all of the work in that area is done by a highly skilled staff of young people, including Armand Aviram, Georgia Parke, Jackson Davis, Kendra Pittman, May Ayad, Chris Moore, and David Shen. I thank them all for what they do.

The goal of our social media effort is not just to promote me and the work I do in the Senate. Mostly, it is to educate the American people about issues that corporate media often ignores. In fact, some of the most viewed videos that we have done don't include me at all.

Our most watched video features a brilliant Canadian doctor, Danielle Martin, responding to distortions about her country's health care being told by Republican senator Richard Burr during a Senate hearing. That video has received more than 30 million views, and it made Dr. Martin a bit of a celebrity in her home country.

As part of our focus on corporate greed, we produced a video that featured a former employee of Amazon, a company owned by the wealthiest person on earth, Jeff Bezos. That employee, Seth King, discussed the terrible working conditions at the Amazon distribution center he worked at. That video received more than 10 million views.

In an unprecedented way, we have also used social media to livestream ninety-minute town hall meetings on some of the most important issues facing our country: Medicare for All, income and wealth inequality, and the Iran nuclear deal. These town hall meetings have been viewed millions of times.

The overall goal of our social media efforts is to educate the American people about the issues that are most relevant to their lives, ones often ignored by corporate media. And I am proud to say that we are succeeding. Since early 2017, videos produced by my office have been viewed more than 1.2 billion times. That's pretty good.

INTRODUCING THE $15-AN-HOUR MINIMUM-WAGE BILL

During the course of my presidential campaign, I stated over and over again that if any person in America works forty hours a week, they should not be living in poverty. That's fair. That's just. That's what a wealthy democratic society should be about.

Unfortunately, that vision is far from today's reality. Sadly, in our current economy, we have tens of millions of people who work forty, fifty, or even sixty hours a week but who continue to struggle to pay for the basic necessities—food, housing, child care, health care, clothing, and transportation. They work hard but fall further and further behind.

I will never forget being at a farmers' market in Des Moines, Iowa, where I met a young man who worked at the local emergency food shelf. He told me that the vast majority of people who came to the food shelf were not unemployed. They were working people who just didn't earn enough to buy the food their families needed. And that is true all over the country. In some areas, where housing is very expensive, full-time employees sleep in their cars or in tents.

At a town hall meeting I held in Detroit, I met with young workers who described what it was like to live on $7.25 an hour working at McDonald's. One young man there was working twenty hours a week in one restaurant, getting on a bus to another McDonald's, and then getting on another bus to a third job. That should not be happening in America, the wealthiest country in the history of the world.

The bottom line is that we need economic policy in this country that improves the lives of all Americans, not just the people on top. While labor productivity has more than doubled since the late 1960s, pay for workers generally and for low-wage workers in particular has either stagnated or fallen since the 1970s. With 52 percent of all new income going to the top 1 percent over the past decade, many workers are now forced to work two or three jobs to survive. They live with incredible stress.

One way to make certain that all Americans have a decent standard of living is to have a minimum wage that is a *living* wage, a wage that allows our lowest-wage workers to live in dignity. Incredibly, despite growing income and wealth inequality, Congress has not passed legislation to increase the federal minimum wage since 2007, and its purchasing power has significantly declined. No one can deny that today's minimum wage of $7.25 per hour is nothing more than a starvation wage. It is time to change that.

On April 26, 2017, I announced that I was introducing legislation that would increase the federal minimum wage from $7.25 an hour to $15 an hour by 2024; thereafter, the minimum wage would be indexed to the median wage. Importantly, this legislation would also eliminate the loophole that allows employers to pay tipped workers—waiters, waitresses, bartenders, barbers, hairdressers, taxi drivers, car wash assistants, and valet parking attendants—a shamefully low $2.13 an hour.

This raise would increase the minimum wage to a purchasing power that would be the highest since 1968. If passed, this bill would give more than 41 million low-wage workers—almost 30 percent of the U.S. workforce—a desperately needed raise. Further, a $15 minimum wage by 2024 would generate $144 billion in higher wages for workers, benefiting their local economies.

Two years ago, I had introduced similar legislation, with five co-sponsors. This time, I had twenty-two senators with me, including most of the Democratic leadership, and we were gaining more cosponsors every day. We were making progress in the fight for economic justice.

Speaking to hundreds of workers at a rally overlooking the U.S. Capitol along with several other senators and members of Congress, I stated, "For the last ten years, Congress, giving tax breaks to the rich, has forgotten to raise the minimum wage. We are here to remind them that a $7.25 minimum wage is a starvation minimum wage. Nobody can live on $7.25. You can't live on $8. You can't live on $10 an hour. And that is why we are saying that after ten years of inaction the United States Congress is going to raise the minimum wage to a living wage: $15 an hour."

That day, Terrance Wise, a McDonald's worker from Kansas City and a leader in the Fight for $15 movement, urged Americans to

think back to five years ago: President Obama had yet to call for even a $9-an-hour federal minimum wage, and the two members of Congress brave enough to call for $10.10 an hour were considered crazy. Then something crazier happened: 200 fast-food workers walked off their jobs in New York City, sparking a movement for $15 an hour and union rights that spread across the country. Twenty-two million Americans now *have won raises totaling $62 billion. We've gone from laughable to inevitable. With today's announcement, it's clear that our Fight for $15 has set a new standard. Democrats across the board support $15 an hour, because they know it's the bare minimum workers like me need to support our families. We're going to keep striking, marching, and speaking out until every worker in the country wins $15 an hour and union rights.*

I couldn't have said it any better myself.

Later that day, Joseph Geevarghese, director of Good Jobs Nation, told the *Huffington Post*, "It is significant that during the week that the nation is marking Trump's first 100 days in office, you're seeing Democrats unify around a common political agenda and at the top of that is a $15 minimum wage bill. . . . This $15 minimum wage bill helps make the economic contrast between Democrats and Republicans, who ran as populists and are governing as business as usual. This is more than we are not the party of Trump, it is we are the party of raising wages and of workers."

When I formally introduced this legislation, on May 25, 2017, at a press conference with Senate Minority Leader Schumer and House Minority Leader Nancy Pelosi, we ended up with thirty original cosponsors.

At the press conference, Representative Pelosi said, "Let's all join the Fight for $15. And I'll tell you one thing for sure: if we win the election, in the first 100 hours, we will pass a $15 minimum wage."

Senator Schumer said, "You can bet Democrats in Congress are going to fight to make $15 minimum wage a reality in this nation, from one end of the country to the other. $15 isn't going to make anybody rich. But it's at least going to let people live a life of dignity. Every American who works hard is entitled to just that."

Raising the minimum wage to $15 an hour may have been a

fringe idea a few years ago, but now it is a mainstream idea whose time has come.

This legislation would also end an outrageous aspect of corporate welfare. Today, many workers in large and profitable corporations, some of which are owned by multibillionaires, earn wages that are so low that they are forced to rely on publicly funded programs like Medicaid, food stamps, and public housing in order to survive. In my view, it is totally absurd for the taxpayers of this country to have to subsidize people like Jeff Bezos, the founder of Amazon and the wealthiest person in the world, worth over $150 billion. He should be paying all his employees a living wage, and a $15-an-hour federal minimum wage would be a step in the right direction toward making that happen.

Like every other important struggle, the "Fight for $15 and a Union" campaign began at the grassroots level when, in 2012, as Terrance Wise said, 200 fast-food workers walked off the job in New York City to demand $15 an hour and union representation. And, with the help of the Service Employees International Union (SEIU), the movement spread. Today, cities across the country, including Seattle; Washington, DC; Minneapolis; San Francisco; Los Angeles; and the states of California and New York, have passed $15-an-hour legislation, and millions of workers have seen substantial wage increases.

We are making progress in the fight for economic justice. The struggle continues.

May 31, 2017

OFF TO GERMANY, ENGLAND, AND IRELAND

In November of 2016, a week after Trump's election, my book *Our Revolution* was published by Thomas Dunne Books. The book described our 2016 insurgent presidential campaign, and then went into some detail regarding how progressive policies could address some of the major crises facing our country. The book sold extremely well, reaching number three on the *New York Times* bestseller list. It was also published in England, Germany, France, China, Serbia, and South Korea.

In the spring of 2017, during the congressional Memorial Day break, I was invited by the European publishers of the book to speak in Germany, England, and Ireland. It was a great opportunity for Jane and me to get away. In addition to meeting some truly wonderful people, we were able to spend time with my brother, Larry, who lives in Oxford, and his family.

The degree to which our 2016 campaign attracted attention throughout the world has never ceased to amaze me. I have received invitations to speak in almost every country in Europe, as well as many countries in Asia, Latin America, and the Middle East. Without being overly modest, I believe that interest has less to do with me than with a profound international fatigue with status quo politics.

All over the world, traditional left parties are in rapid decline. Facing major crises, these parties have not responded effectively. The old political leadership and their ideas have grown stale and have alienated working-class and young people who have historically supported them. In an increasingly complicated and uncaring world, people are searching for meaning and community. They want to make a difference. They want real change and a better world for themselves and their children. They are prepared to take on powerful special interests and get involved. Our campaign, and the energy, hope, and excitement it created, lit a spark of interest in countries throughout the world.

My trip to Europe attracted even more attention than it would normally have because of the ascendancy of Trump to the presidency. There was enormous curiosity and concern there about what was now going on in America. Did Trump really reflect the views of the American people, or was he an aberration? Where was the American government going to lead the world?

The people of Europe, for a variety of reasons, were very fond of President Obama. They were very, very wary about Donald Trump and were eager to hear from an American politician who shared their concerns. And that was me.

Our first stop was Germany, where I gave a public address at the Free University of Berlin. Frankly, I was overwhelmed and humbled by the greeting I received. I was also impressed by the knowledge that so many in the audience had about American politics, my campaign, and my views. As *Newsweek* reported, "Just days after Trump received a frosty reception on his first trip across the

Atlantic since entering the White House, Sanders earned a rap-
turous reception from more than 1,000 students at Berlin's Free
University Wednesday."

The article continued: "Sanders . . . has long been popular in
Europe. In the Democratic primary against Hillary Clinton, he
won more than 60 percent of the vote in Germany, France, Spain,
and the United Kingdom. The reasons for that popularity are not
hard to fathom. Sanders' socialist policies are far more mainstream
in Europe than in the United States. In particular, his call for universal health care, while deemed a far-left fantasy by even some
Democrats in the U.S., is the norm in Europe and even supported
by conservative parties."

I told the crowd, "Trump does not reflect the values of most
Americans and we look forward, despite what happened last week
here, we absolutely look forward to working with the great people
of Germany, with Europe, the UK. Our job is to bring people
around the world together and not create fights when they're not
necessary."

It was pointed out that my remarks in Berlin had a bit of historical context. In June 1963, President John F. Kennedy gave a
major speech just outside the auditorium where I spoke. I was
proud to have followed in his footsteps in speaking about the
need for U.S.-European unity.

And then it was on to England, where I spoke in Brighton, Cambridge, Oxford, London, and Bristol. It was kind of like a political
campaign. Except, this time I wasn't asking for votes. I was asking
for international cooperation to address some of the major crises
facing our planet. At every venue, the crowds were large and en-
thusiastic.

While I was not in Europe to campaign, that doesn't mean there
wasn't a very hotly contested election going on. In fact, I walked

right into the middle of it. The general election in the UK was scheduled for June 8, just a few days after I was to leave that country. While the Conservatives were expected to retain control of Parliament, the Labour Party, under socialist Jeremy Corbyn, was putting up a much stronger show of opposition than had been expected, and their campaign had real momentum. During my stay in the UK, I was asked time and again about my views on the election. While I strongly supported Labour and was very impressed by the grassroots activism I was seeing, I didn't think it would be of help to them to have an American getting involved. So I politely demurred comment.

On June 2, I spoke to the Oxford Union at Oxford University. The *Oxford Student*, the university newspaper, gave an account of the visit, writing:

"Many in the audience had been queuing for hours, and when finally the Senator arrived in the chamber he was greeted with a thunderous, standing ovation and a chorus of cheering.

"By contrast, Sanders was quick to get down to business, muttering a word of thanks to the audience before immediately launching into a stinging criticism of Donald Trump."

I told the Oxford audience, "I know there has been a lot of concern about what is happening in America, but I just want you to know that his views are not shared by the majority of the American people."

The *Oxford Union* reported that I ended my speech stating, "If I had told you thirty years ago that we would have an African American president, you would have laughed. If I had told you gay marriage would be legal across the whole of America, you would have laughed too."

They also noted that I asked students to join the fight: "We need your energy, your enthusiasm. We need your courage."

Ireland is one of the most beautiful countries on earth. It very much reminds me of Vermont, with the added benefit of having an ocean. It is also where Jane's family comes from. I was delighted, therefore, to speak at the Dalkey Book Festival in Dublin after we left England, where our host was the well-known Irish journalist and economist David McWilliams. Frankly, I was a bit stunned to learn that tickets to the event, in a rather large auditorium, were sold out in under five minutes, and that at one point the event's website crashed due to the sheer volume of users trying to access it.

In my remarks in Ireland, I stressed the strong historical ties that our two countries had and the need for both countries to continue working together to retain and expand our democratic values. I also indicated my support for those in Ireland who were attempting to end the ban on abortion.

While in Dublin, we also had the opportunity to meet with the president of the country, Michael D. Higgins, a poet, philosopher, and strong progressive, in his beautiful official residence in Phoenix Park. While there, I gave him a copy of my new book, and he gave me a copy of his. We had a great discussion about almost every subject under the sun.

Jane is a genealogy buff and has spent a lot of time tracing her family roots. Earlier in the day, she had been enormously excited to meet with two of the leading genealogists in Ireland, who had researched her family history. To her surprise, she was presented with small pieces of the remaining wall of her great-great-grandparents' home in Youghal, in County Cork. Trust me. At the proper time, they will be given to our grandchildren for safekeeping.

The brief trip to Europe was not only a success in terms of the wonderfully large turnouts we had and the strong showing of support we received. To me, what was most important was the reaffirmation of international solidarity. It was very comforting and gratifying to know that, on both sides of the Atlantic, good people would continue to oppose bigotry and divisiveness and strive for a world of peace and justice. I came back to Washington feeling better and more confident about the state of the world than when I left.

A PROGRESSIVE FOREIGN POLICY

During my presidential campaign, I had been criticized for not speaking out enough on foreign policy. That criticism was heightened by the fact that I was running against a former secretary of state, someone who had traveled the globe meeting foreign leaders and was considered to be one of the leading experts in our country on international affairs.

There was no question that Hillary Clinton had a lot more experience than I had on foreign policy matters, but that did not mean that her foreign policy record or judgment was better than mine. It wasn't.

As I made clear in my debates against her, and in other opportunities over the years, I had as a young man strongly opposed the disastrous war in Vietnam, one of the worst foreign policy blunders in the history of our country. I had also spoken out against U.S. coups and invasions that overthrew democratically elected governments in Chile, Guatemala, the Congo, Brazil, Iran, and elsewhere.

As a freshman congressman in 1991, I voted against the first

Persian Gulf War, which laid the groundwork for our future involvement in the Gulf. In one of my earliest speeches in Congress, I went to the House floor and said, "Despite the fact that we are now aligned with such Middle Eastern governments as Syria, a terrorist dictatorship, Saudi Arabia and Kuwait, feudalistic dictatorships, and Egypt, a one-party state that receives $7 billion in debt forgiveness to wage this war with us, I believe that, in the long run, the action unleashed last night will go strongly against our interests in the Middle East. Clearly, the United States and allies will win this war, but the death and destruction caused will, in my opinion, not be forgotten by the poor people of the Third World and the people of the Middle East in particular . . . I fear that one day we will regret that decision and that we are in fact laying the groundwork for more and more wars in that region for years to come." Not a bad analysis for a freshman congressman.

In 2003, I did everything I could to prevent George W. Bush's invasion of Iraq—a war that Clinton supported. In one debate, when Hillary Clinton cited Henry Kissinger as a friend and mentor, I suggested that he was a terrible secretary of state, a war criminal, and would play no role in a Sanders administration.

The first Iraq War did lay the groundwork for more wars to come. This, of course, is the result of U.S. foreign policy meddling, in particular in the Middle East. As part of our Cold War efforts, we overthrew the democratically elected prime minister of Iran, Mohammad Mossadegh in 1953, and installed the Shah, a brutal dictator. This led to the Islamic Revolution, the rise of the Ayatollah Khomeini, the taking of hostages at the U.S. embassy, and our current hostile relationship with Iran.

Ultimately, the first war in Iraq led to a second war in Iraq, which led to the rise of ISIS. Our foreign policy actions have consequences and reverberate for decades into the future. Let me be clear: I am not a pacifist. I do believe that military force can be a necessary tool when applied in appropriate circumstances. The question is when that should be.

From my time as mayor of Burlington, I believed it was critical that Americans reach out and play a constructive role in the world community. That is why, as mayor, I did what very few mayors do: develop a municipal foreign policy under the banner of "think globally, act locally." I traveled to Nicaragua to oppose U.S. efforts to overthrow the Sandinista government and helped create a sister-city relationship with a town there called Puerto Cabezas. Along with a delegation of Burlingtonians, I also visited what was then the Soviet Union and helped establish a sister-city program there with Yaroslavl.

I believed then and believe today that people reaching out to people, forming bonds and connecting, is the beginning of understanding and peace. I will never forget high school students from Yaroslavl, part of a country that was then our major enemy, walking in a Burlington park with kids from Vermont. They were having a great time. It was hard to tell the kids from our "enemy" country from the locals.

As the summer approached, I received an invitation to speak at Westminster College in Fulton, Missouri, on September 21, 2017, when I would also receive an honorary degree. This tiny university has a unique place in history as the site of Winston Churchill's famous "Iron Curtain" speech. Following that speech, a parade of world leaders have visited the college to share their thoughts, including Harry Truman, George H. W. Bush, and Margaret Thatcher.

I accepted the very kind invitation from Westminster College because it presented a unique opportunity to lay out what I meant by a "progressive foreign policy." Because much of the focus of my career has been on domestic issues like the economy and health

care, there is the false assumption that foreign policy is not important to me. That is just not right. The truth is that some of the
most consequential, difficult, and gut-wrenching votes I have ever
taken as a member of Congress focused on our country's place in
the world, something I worried deeply about.

When I left Washington for Missouri the afternoon before the
speech, I had a draft in my hands, which was not quite ready. It
needed more work. It was going to be a long night of writing.

When I and two staff members arrived at Fulton in the evening, and before we could get to work on the speech, we were given
a quick tour of the beautiful campus, which clearly celebrates its role
in history. The tiny gym where Churchill delivered his address
remains, with reminders of the Churchill visit, and the grounds are
decorated with several large pieces of the Berlin Wall. The campus
also hosts the National Churchill Museum.

My staff and I spent the night across from the campus, at a historic bed-and-breakfast where, among others, Margaret Thatcher
stayed during her visit to campus. One of my staff members, Ari
Rabin-Havt, stayed in the bed Thatcher slept in, while I opted for
a room across the hall.

After our campus tour, and with a plateful of cookies on the
table left by our very gracious hostess, Ari; Matt Duss, my foreign
policy adviser; and I worked together into the early-morning hours,
poring over the remarks and rewriting much of the draft. Our goal
was ambitious: to draft a speech defining what I believed to be a
progressive role in the world for the United States while addressing the immediate crises we faced.

Here is the speech I delivered:

Let me begin by thanking Westminster College, which year
after year invites political leaders to discuss the important

issue of foreign policy and America's role in the world. I am honored to be here today and I thank you very much for the invitation.

One of the reasons I accepted the invitation to speak here is that I strongly believe that not only do we need to begin a more vigorous debate about foreign policy; we also need to broaden our understanding of what foreign policy is.

So let me be clear: Foreign policy is directly related to military policy and has everything to do with almost seven thousand young Americans being killed in Iraq and Afghanistan, and tens of thousands coming home wounded in body and spirit from a war we should never have started. That's foreign policy. And foreign policy is about hundreds of thousands of people in Iraq and Afghanistan dying in that same war.

Foreign policy is about U.S. government budget priorities. At a time when we already spend more on defense than the next ten nations combined, foreign policy is about authorizing a defense budget of some $700 billion, including a $50 billion increase passed just last week.

Meanwhile, at the exact same time as the president and many of my Republican colleagues want to substantially increase military spending, they want to throw 32 million Americans off of the health insurance they currently have because, supposedly, they are worried about the budget deficit. While greatly increasing military spending they also want to cut education, environmental protection, and the needs of children and seniors.

Foreign policy, therefore, is remembering what Dwight D. Eisenhower said as he left office: "In the councils of government, we must guard against the acquisition of unwarranted influence, whether sought or unsought, by the military-industrial complex. The potential for the disastrous rise of misplaced power exists and will persist."

And he also reminded us that "every gun that is made, every warship launched, every rocket fired signifies, in the final sense, a theft from those who hunger and are not fed, those who are cold and are not clothed. This world in arms is not spending money alone. It is spending the sweat of its laborers, the genius of its scientists, the hopes of its children. The cost of one modern heavy bomber is this: a modern brick school in more than thirty cities. It is two electric power plants, each serving a town of 60,000 population. It is two fine, fully equipped hospitals. It is some fifty miles of concrete highway . . ."

What Eisenhower said over fifty years ago is even more true today.

Foreign policy is about whether we continue to champion the values of freedom, democracy, and justice, values which have been a beacon of hope for people throughout the world, or whether we support undemocratic, repressive regimes, which torture, jail, and deny basic rights to their citizens.

What foreign policy also means is that if we are going to expound the virtues of democracy and justice abroad, and be taken seriously, we need to practice those values here at home. That means continuing the struggle to end racism, sexism, xenophobia, and homophobia here in the United States and making it clear that when people in America march on our streets as neo-Nazis or white supremacists, we have no ambiguity in condemning everything they stand for. There are no two sides on that issue.

Foreign policy is not just tied into military affairs; it is directly connected to economics. Foreign policy must take into account the outrageous income and wealth inequality that exists globally and in our own country. This planet will not be secure or peaceful when so few have so much, and so many have so little—and when we advance day after day into an oligarchic form of society where a small number of extraordinarily powerful special interests exert enormous influence over the economic and political life of the world.

There is no moral or economic justification for the six wealthiest people in the world having as much wealth as the bottom half of the world's population—3.7 billion people. There is no justification for the incredible power and dominance that Wall Street, giant multinational corporations, and international financial institutions have over the affairs of sovereign countries throughout the world.

At a time when climate change is causing devastating problems here in America and around the world, foreign policy is about whether we work with the international community—with China, Russia, India, and countries around the world—to transform our energy systems away from fossil fuel to energy efficiency and sustainable energy. Sensible foreign policy understands that climate change is a real threat to every country on earth, that it is not a hoax, and that no country alone can effectively combat it. It is an issue for the entire international community, and an issue that the United States should be leading in, not ignoring or denying.

My point is that we need to look at foreign policy as more than just the crisis of the day. That is important, but we need a more expansive view.

Almost seventy years ago, former British prime minister

Winston Churchill stood on this stage and gave an historic address, known as the "Iron Curtain" speech, in which he framed a conception of world affairs that endured through the twentieth century, until the collapse of the Soviet Union. In that speech, he defined his strategic concept as "nothing less than the safety and welfare, the freedom and progress, of all the homes and families of all the men and women in all the lands.

"To give security to these countless homes," he said, "they must be shielded from the two giant marauders, war and tyranny."

How do we meet that challenge today? How do we fight now for the "freedom and progress" that Churchill talked about then? At a time of exploding technology and wealth, how do we move away from a world of war, terrorism, and massive levels of poverty into a world of peace and economic security for all? How do we move toward a global community in which people have the decent jobs, food, clean water, education, health care, and housing they need? These are, admittedly, not easy issues to deal with, but they are questions we cannot afford to ignore.

At the outset, I think it is important to recognize that the world of today is very, very different from the world of Winston Churchill of 1946. Back then we faced a superpower adversary with a huge standing army, with an arsenal of nuclear weapons, with allies around the world, and with expansionist aims. Today the Soviet Union no longer exists.

Today we face threats of a different sort. We will never forget 9/11. We are cognizant of the terrible attacks that have taken place in capitals all over the world. We are more than aware of the brutality of ISIS, Al Qaeda, and similar groups.

We also face the threat of these groups obtaining weapons of mass destruction, and preventing that must be a priority.

In recent years, we are increasingly confronted by the isolated dictatorship of North Korea, which is making rapid progress in nuclear weaponry and intercontinental ballistic missiles.

Yes, we face real and very serious threats to our security, which I will discuss, but they are very different than what we have seen in the past, and our response must be equally different.

But before I talk about some of these other threats, let me say a few words about a very insidious challenge that undermines our ability to meet these other crises, and indeed could undermine our very way of life.

A great concern that I have today is that many in our country are losing faith in our common future and in our democratic values. For far too many of our people, here in the United States and people all over the world, the promises of self-government—of government by the people, for the people, and of the people—have not been kept. And people are losing faith.

In the United States and other countries, a majority of people are working longer hours for lower wages than they used to. They see big money buying elections, and they see a political and economic elite growing wealthier, even as their own children's future grows dimmer.

So when we talk about foreign policy, and our belief in democracy, at the very top of our list of concerns is the need to revitalize American democracy to ensure that governmental decisions reflect the interests of a majority of our people, and not just the few—whether that few is Wall

Street, the military-industrial complex, or the fossil fuel industry. We cannot convincingly promote democracy abroad if we do not live it vigorously here at home.

Maybe it's because I come from the small state of Vermont, a state that prides itself on town hall meetings and grassroots democracy, that I strongly agree with Winston Churchill, who believed that "democracy is the worst form of government, except for all those other forms."

In both Europe and the United States, the international order that the United States helped establish over the past seventy years, one that put great emphasis on democracy and human rights, and which promoted greater trade and economic development, is under great strain. Many Europeans are questioning the value of the European Union. Many Americans are questioning the value of the United Nations, of the transatlantic alliance, and of other multilateral organizations.

We also see a rise in authoritarianism and right-wing extremism—both domestic and foreign—which further weakens this order by exploiting and amplifying resentments, stoking intolerance, and fanning ethnic and racial hatreds among those in our societies who are struggling.

We saw this antidemocratic effort in the 2016 election, right here in the United States, where we now know that the Russian government was engaged in a massive effort to undermine two of our greatest strengths: the integrity of our elections, and our faith in our own democracy.

I found it incredible, by the way, that when the president of the United States spoke before the United Nations . . . he did not even mention that outrage.

Well, I will. Today I say to Mr. Putin: We will not allow

you to undermine American democracy or democracies around the world. In fact, our goal is to not only strengthen American democracy, but to work in solidarity with supporters of democracy around the globe, including in Russia. In the struggle of democracy versus authoritarianism, we intend to win.

When we talk about foreign policy, it is clear that there are some who believe that the United States would be best served by withdrawing from the global community. I disagree. As the wealthiest and most powerful nation on earth, we have got to help lead the struggle to defend and expand a rules-based international order in which law, not might, makes right.

We must offer people a vision that one day, maybe not in our lifetimes, but one day in the future, human beings on this planet will live in a world where international conflicts will be resolved peacefully, not by mass murder.

How tragic it is that today, while hundreds of millions of people live in abysmal poverty, the arms merchants of the world grow increasingly rich as governments spend trillions of dollars on weapons of destruction.

I am not naïve or unmindful of history. Many of the conflicts that plague our world are long-standing and complex. But we must never lose our vision of a world in which, to quote the prophet Isaiah, "they shall beat their swords into plowshares, and their spears into pruning hooks: nation shall not lift up sword against nation, neither shall they learn war anymore."

One of the most important organizations for promoting a vision of a different world is the United Nations. Former First

Lady Eleanor Roosevelt, who helped create the UN, called it "our greatest hope for future peace. Alone we cannot keep the peace of the world, but in cooperation with others we have to achieve this much longed-for security."

It has become fashionable to bash the UN. And yes, the UN needs to be reformed. It can be ineffective, bureaucratic, too slow or unwilling to act, even in the face of massive atrocities, as we are seeing in Syria right now. But to see only its weaknesses is to overlook the enormously important work the UN does in promoting global health, aiding refugees, and monitoring elections, and in international peacekeeping missions, among other things. All of these activities contribute to reduced conflict, to wars that don't have to be ended because they never start.

At the end of the day, it is obvious that it makes far more sense to have a forum in which countries can debate their concerns, and work out compromises and agreements. Dialogue and debate are far preferable to bombs, poison gas, and war.

Dialogue, however, cannot take place only between foreign ministers or diplomats at the United Nations. It should be taking place between people throughout the world at the grassroots level.

When I was mayor of Burlington in the 1980s, the Soviet Union was our enemy. We established a sister-city program with the Russian city of Yaroslavl, a program that still exists today. I will never forget seeing Russian boys and girls visiting Vermont, getting to know American kids, and becoming good friends. Hatred and wars are often based on fear and ignorance. The way to defeat this ignorance and diminish this fear is through meeting with others and understanding the way they see the world. Good foreign policy means building people-to-people relationships.

We should welcome young people from all over the world and from all walks of life to spend time with our kids in American classrooms, while our kids, from all income levels, do the same abroad.

Some in Washington continue to argue that "benevolent global hegemony" should be the goal of our foreign policy, that the United States, by virtue of its extraordinary military power, should stand astride the world and reshape it to its liking. I would argue that the events of the past two decades—particularly the disastrous Iraq War and the instability and destruction it has brought to the region—have utterly discredited that vision.

The goal is not for the United States to dominate the world. Nor, on the other hand, is our goal to withdraw from the international community and shirk our responsibilities under the banner of "America First." Our goal should be global engagement based on partnership rather than dominance. This is better for our security, better for global stability, and better for facilitating the international cooperation necessary to meet shared challenges.

Here's a truth that you don't often hear about in the newspapers, on television, or in the halls of Congress. But it's a truth we must face. Far too often, American intervention and the use of American military power have produced unintended consequences that have caused incalculable harm. Yes, it is reasonably easy to engineer the overthrow of a government. It is far harder, however, to know the long-term impact that that action will have. Let me give you some examples:

In 1953 the United States, on behalf of Western oil interests, supported the overthrow of Mohammad Mossadegh, Iran's elected prime minister, and the reinstallation of the shah of Iran, who led a corrupt, brutal, and unpopular government. In 1979, the shah was overthrown by revolutionaries led by Ayatollah Khomeini, and the Islamic Republic of Iran was created. What would Iran look like today if their democratic government had not been overthrown? What impact did that American-led coup have on the entire region? What consequences are we still living with today?

In 1973, the United States supported the coup against the democratically elected president of Chile, Salvador Allende, which was led by General Augusto Pinochet. The result was almost twenty years of authoritarian military rule and the disappearance and torture of thousands of Chileans—and the intensification of anti-Americanism in Latin America.

Elsewhere in Latin America, the logic of the Cold War led the United States to support murderous regimes in El Salvador and Guatemala, which resulted in brutal and long-lasting civil wars that killed hundreds of thousands of innocent men, women, and children.

In Vietnam, based on a discredited "domino theory," the United States replaced the French in intervening in a civil war, which resulted in the deaths of millions of Vietnamese in support of a corrupt, repressive South Vietnamese government. We must never forget that over 58,000 Americans also died in that war.

More recently, in Iraq, based on a similarly mistaken analysis of the threat posed by Saddam Hussein's regime, the United States invaded and occupied a country in the heart of the Middle East. In doing so, we upended the regional order of the Middle East and unleashed forces across the region and the world that we'll be dealing with for decades to come.

These are just a few examples of American foreign policy and interventionism that proved to be counterproductive.

Now let me give you an example of an incredibly bold and ambitious American initiative that proved to be enormously successful and in which not one bullet was fired—something that we must learn from.

Shortly after Churchill was right here in Westminster College, the United States developed an extremely radical foreign policy initiative called the Marshall Plan.

Think about it for a moment: historically, when countries won terrible wars, they exacted retribution on the vanquished. But in 1948, the United States government did something absolutely unprecedented. After losing hundreds of thousands of soldiers in the most brutal war in history to defeat the barbarity of Nazi Germany and Japanese imperialism, the government of the United States decided not to punish and humiliate the losers. Rather, we helped rebuild their economies, spending the equivalent of $130 billion just to reconstruct Western Europe after World War II. We also provided them support to reconstruct democratic societies.

That program was an amazing success. Today Germany, the country of the Holocaust, the country of Hitler's dictatorship, is now a strong democracy and the economic engine of Europe. Despite centuries of hostility, there has not been a major European war since World War II. That is an extraordinary foreign policy success that we have every right to be very proud of.

Unfortunately, today we still have examples of the United States supporting policies that I believe will come back to haunt us. One is the ongoing Saudi war in Yemen.

While we rightly condemn Russian and Iranian support for Bashar al-Assad's slaughter in Syria, the United States continues to support Saudi Arabia's destructive intervention in Yemen, which has killed many thousands of civilians and created a humanitarian crisis in one of the region's poorest countries. Such policies dramatically undermine America's ability to advance a human rights agenda around the world, and empowers authoritarian leaders who insist that our support for those rights and values is not serious.

Let me say a word about some of the shared global challenges that we face today.

First, I would mention climate change. Friends, it is time to get serious on this: climate change is real and must be addressed with the full weight of American power, attention, and resources.

The scientific community is virtually unanimous in telling us that climate change is real, climate change is caused by human activity, and climate change is already causing devastating harm throughout the world. Further, what the scientists tell us is that if we do not act boldly to address the climate crisis, this planet will see more drought, more floods—the recent devastation by Hurricanes Harvey and Irma are good examples—more extreme weather disturbances, more acidification of the ocean, more rising sea levels, and, as a result of mass migrations, there will be more threats to global stability and security.

President Trump's decision to withdraw from the Paris Agreement was not only incredibly foolish and shortsighted, but it will also end up hurting the American economy.

The threat of climate change is a very clear example of where American leadership can make a difference. Europe can't do it alone, China can't do it alone, and the United States can't do it alone. This is a crisis that calls out for strong international cooperation if we are to leave our children and grandchildren a planet that is healthy and habitable. American leadership—the economic and scientific advantages and incentives that only America can offer—is hugely important for facilitating this cooperation.

Another challenge that we and the entire world face is growing wealth and income inequality, and the movement toward international oligarchy—a system in which a small number of billionaires and corporate interests have control over our economic life, our political life, and our media. This movement toward oligarchy is not just an American issue. It is an international issue. Globally, the top 1 percent now owns more wealth than the bottom 99 percent of the world's population.

In other words, while the very, very rich become much richer, thousands of children die every week in poor countries around the world from easily prevented diseases, and hundreds of millions live in incredible squalor.

Inequality, corruption, oligarchy, and authoritarianism are inseparable. They must be understood as part of the same system, and fought in the same way. Around the world we have witnessed the rise of demagogues who, once in power, use their positions to loot the state of its resources. These kleptocrats, like Putin in Russia, use divisiveness and abuse as a tool for enriching themselves and those loyal to them.

But economic inequality is not the only form of inequality that we must face. As we seek to renew America's commitment to promote human rights and human dignity around the world we must be a living example here at home. We must reject the divisive attacks based on a person's religion, race, gender, sexual orientation or identity, country of origin, or class. And when we see demonstrations of neo-Nazism and white supremacism as we recently did in Charlottesville, Virginia, we must be unequivocal in our condemnation, as our president shamefully was not.

And as we saw here so clearly in St. Louis in the past week we need serious reforms in policing and the criminal justice system so that the life of every person is equally valued and protected. We cannot speak with the moral authority the world needs if we do not struggle to achieve the ideal we are holding out for others.

One of the places we have fallen short in upholding these ideas is in the war on terrorism. Here I want to be clear: terrorism is a very real threat, as we learned so tragically on September 11, 2001, and many other countries have experienced similar attacks.

But, I also want to be clear about something else: as an organizing framework, the global war on terror has been a disaster for the American people and for American leadership. Orienting U.S. national security strategy around terrorism essentially allowed a few thousand violent extremists to dictate policy for the most powerful nation on earth. It responds to terrorists by giving them exactly what they want.

In addition to draining our resources and distorting our vision, the war on terror has caused us to undermine our own moral standards regarding torture, indefinite detention, and the use of force around the world, using drone strikes and other airstrikes that often result in high civilian casualties.

A heavy-handed military approach, with little transparency or accountability, doesn't enhance our security. It makes the problem worse.

We must rethink the old Washington mind-set that judges "seriousness" according to the willingness to use force. One of the key misapprehensions of this mind-set is the idea that military force is decisive in a way that diplomacy is not.

Yes, military force is sometimes necessary, but always— always—as the last resort. And blustery threats of force, while they might make a few columnists happy, can often signal weakness as much as strength, diminishing U.S. deterrence, credibility, and security in the process.

To illustrate this, I would contrast two recent U.S. foreign policy initiatives: The Iraq War and the Iran nuclear agreement.

Today it is now broadly acknowledged that the war in Iraq, which I opposed, was a foreign policy blunder of enormous magnitude. In addition to the many thousands killed, it created a cascade of instability around the region that we are still dealing with today in Syria and elsewhere, and will be for many years to come. Indeed, had it not been for the Iraq War, ISIS would almost certainly not exist. The Iraq War, as I said before, had unintended consequences. It was intended as a demonstration of the extent of American power. It ended up demonstrating only its limits.

In contrast, the Iran nuclear deal advanced the security of the U.S. and its partners, and it did this at a cost of no blood and zero treasure.

For many years, leaders across the world had become increasingly concerned about the possibility of an Iranian nuclear weapon. What the Obama administration and our European allies were able to do was to get an agreement that froze and dismantled large parts of that nuclear program, put it under the most intensive inspections regime in history, and removed the prospect of an Iranian nuclear weapon from the list of global threats.

That is real leadership. That is real power.

Just yesterday, the top general of U.S. Strategic Command, General John Hyten, said, "The facts are that Iran is operating under the agreements that we signed up for." We now have a four-year record of Iran's compliance, going back to the 2013 interim deal.

I call on my colleagues in the Congress, and all Americans: we must protect this deal. President Trump has signaled his intention to walk away from it, as he did the Paris Agreement, regardless of the evidence that it is working. That would be a mistake.

Not only would this potentially free Iran from the limits placed on its nuclear program; it would irreparably harm America's ability to negotiate future nonproliferation agreements. Why would any country in the world sign such an agreement with the United States if they knew that a reckless president and an irresponsible Congress might simply discard that agreement a few years later?

If we are genuinely concerned with Iran's behavior in the region, as I am, the worst possible thing we could do is break the nuclear deal. It would make all of these other problems harder.

Another problem it would make harder is that of North Korea. Let's understand: North Korea is ruled by one of the worst regimes in the world. For many years, its leadership has sacrificed the well-being of its own people in order to develop nuclear weapons and missile programs in order to protect the Kim family's regime. Their continued development of nuclear weapons and missile capability is a growing threat to the U.S. and our allies. Despite past efforts they have repeatedly shown their determination to move forward with these programs in defiance of virtually unanimous international opposition and condemnation.

As we saw with the 2015 nuclear agreement with Iran, real U.S. leadership is shown by our ability to develop consensus around shared problems, and mobilize that consensus toward a solution. That is the model we should be pursuing with North Korea.

As we did with Iran, if North Korea continues to refuse to negotiate seriously, we should look for ways to tighten international sanctions. This will involve working closely with other countries, particularly China, on whom North Korea relies for some 80 percent of its trade. But we should also continue to make clear that this is a shared problem, not to be solved by any one country alone but by the international community working together.

An approach that really uses all the tools of our power—political, economic, civil society—to encourage other states to adopt more inclusive governance will ultimately make us safer.

Development aid is not charity; it advances our national security. It's worth noting that the U.S. military is a stalwart supporter of non-defense diplomacy and development aid.

Starving diplomacy and aid now will result in greater defense needs later on.

U.S. foreign aid should be accompanied by stronger emphasis on helping people gain their political and civil rights to hold oppressive governments accountable to the people. Ultimately, governments that are accountable to the needs of their people will make more dependable partners.

Here is the bottom line: in my view, the United States must seek partnerships not just between governments, but between peoples. A sensible and effective foreign policy recognizes that our safety and welfare is bound up with the safety and welfare of others around the world, with "all the homes and families of all the men and women in all the lands," as Churchill said right here, seventy years ago.

In my view, every person on this planet shares a common humanity. We all want our children to grow up healthy, to have a good education, have decent jobs, drink clean water and breathe clean air, and to live in peace. That's what being human is about.

Our job is to build on that common humanity and do everything that we can to oppose all of the forces, whether unaccountable government power or unaccountable corporate power, who try to divide us up and set us against each other. As Eleanor Roosevelt reminded us, "The world of the future is in our making. Tomorrow is now."

My friends, let us go forward and build that tomorrow.

My speech received a lot of positive attention for broadening the discussion about new options for foreign policy. Robert Borosage, of the *Nation*, wrote:

> *Senator Bernie Sanders received rapturous applause from progressives for his foreign-policy speech at Westminster College in Fulton, Missouri, last week. "One of the finest speeches of his career,"* wrote the Nation's *John Nichols. "The progressive foreign policy speech we've been waiting for," said Stephen Miles. Jacob Heilbrunn, of the more conservative* National Interest, *suggested that Sanders was bringing "regime change" to the liberal interventionism of the Democratic establishment. The reaction was understandable: The speech was like a thunderclap breaking the silence of any serious foreign-policy challenge from the left.*

I VISIT PUERTO RICO

On the morning of Wednesday, September 20, 2017, Hurricane Maria struck Puerto Rico. This was the most devastating storm to hit the island in eighty years, and it plunged its 3.4 million residents into an unprecedented humanitarian crisis. Millions of people lost their jobs and income, their electricity, their clean water supply, their cell phone service, their access to health care, and their ability to go to school. And it turned out that 2,978 people were killed in Puerto Rico and the U.S. Virgin Islands, one more than the number of people murdered on 9/11.

The people of Puerto Rico, like the people of the U.S. Virgin Islands, are full American citizens. Unfortunately, their political status as a U.S. "territory" denies them meaningful representation in Washington. They are not able to vote in the general election for president of the United States. They have one nonvoting member in the U.S. House and no members in the U.S. Senate. Given that lack of political clout, I intended to do everything I could to make sure that the citizens of Puerto Rico received the same kind of response from the federal government as would the citizens of any state in the country.

The truth of the matter is, however, that the economic and political crisis in Puerto Rico goes back a lot further than the devastation wrought by Hurricane Maria. It is about a long history of colonialism and exploitation that gets very little public attention, and which few people on the mainland know much about.

During my presidential campaign in 2016, I not only visited Puerto Rico but met with leaders of the Puerto Rican community who were living in New York and elsewhere. And I learned a lot. As a result, I spoke about the tragic reality that, since 2006, Puerto Rico had lost 20 percent of its jobs, and that about 60 percent of Puerto Rico's adult population were either unemployed or had given up looking for work. In other words, Puerto Rico remained in the midst of a major and prolonged depression.

I talked about how, over the last five years alone, more than 150 public schools had been shut down, and how the childhood poverty rate had shot up to 57 percent. At a time when the rich are getting richer throughout the United States, Puerto Rico now has more income inequality than any state in the country.

As a result of its economic crisis, the Puerto Rican government was deep in debt and heading toward bankruptcy. Wall Street institutions, sensing the opportunity to make a killing at the expense of a weak and impoverished territory, were there to "help." They lent the government money at usurious interest rates, making a terrible economic situation even worse as the government faced the option of feeding hungry children, keeping schools open, or paying off greedy Wall Street creditors.

In 2015, Puerto Rico owed over $70 billion and was paying, in some cases, a 34 percent interest rate on tax-exempt bonds that vulture capitalists purchased at 29 cents on the dollar. It was my strong position that the people of Puerto Rico should not be forced to suffer even more in order that a handful of wealthy investors could make outrageous profits. I called on those investors to take a major "haircut" and understand that they could not get blood from a stone and make huge profits off a deeply impoverished and suffering island.

Unfortunately, the business model of Wall Street is not about compassion, honesty, or decency. They were determined to get their blood money.

Then Maria hit.

Five weeks later, I visited Puerto Rico. I had been very impressed by how the mayor of San Juan, Carmen Yulín Cruz, was handling the crisis, and by her willingness to stand up to Trump's lies as to how effective the Federal Emergency Management Agency (FEMA) had performed during the crisis. I was happy, therefore, to accept her invitation and to see how we could best work together.

As I said at a press conference we held together in San Juan, "The reason I am here today is to listen, and to hear from the people of Puerto Rico about how we address the immediate set of crises that the island faces short term."

During my trip, I was able to walk the streets with the mayor and get a firsthand account from residents about what they were experiencing. I saw the destroyed homes and damaged infrastructure. I talked to people who had no electricity, no refrigeration, no drinkable water. I saw the extensive relief efforts that the city and FEMA were involved with, and met with workers who were getting emergency food and water to people whose lives depended upon that help. I was also able to hold a town hall meeting, where I met with teachers, trade unionists, students, local officials, and others—people whose voices had not been heard.

My goal in taking the trip was not only to personally learn as much as possible about the reality of conditions in Puerto Rico but to make certain that the media continued to pay attention to the crisis there. As a disaster relief bill was coming up shortly in Congress, I wanted to make sure that Puerto Rico's legitimate needs were recognized and addressed, and that the island was treated as fairly as Florida, which had also been hard hit by Maria, and Texas, which had been devastated by Hurricane Harvey in August.

While in San Juan, I also stressed that it would be absolutely absurd and counterproductive simply to rebuild Puerto Rico to where it was before the storm. There was no sense, for example, in rebuilding an electrical infrastructure that was expensive and inefficient, while not taking advantage of the ample supply of solar and wind energy available. It would be equally stupid to replace destroyed housing without making certain that the new structures were storm-resistant.

Visiting Puerto Rico several weeks after the hurricane was an interesting political experience. The politics on the island are difficult and complicated, and I absolutely did not want to get caught in the middle of them. My job was to focus on disaster relief and how we could be most helpful to the people of Puerto Rico.

My visit was hosted by Mayor Cruz, which was apparently of concern to the governor, who was of a different political party. He also wanted to chat with me during what had already become a very tightly scheduled day. A back-and-forth took place between my staff and the governor's office about possible times we could meet yielded no conclusion. The interesting resolution of that problem took place when, after I landed at the airport and got into the mayor's car, we were pulled over on the way to San Juan by several police cars, lights flashing, from the governor's office. And there, on the side of the road, with cars whizzing by, is where the governor and I had our pleasant meeting, photographers and all.

On November 28, 2017, I introduced a $146 billion recovery plan backed by Cruz to address both the short-term and long-term needs of Puerto Rico and the Virgin Islands, which were also devastated by Maria. As I said when I introduced the bill, "It is unconscionable that in the wealthiest nation in the world we have allowed our fellow citizens to suffer for so long. The full resources of the United States must be brought to bear on this crisis, for as long as is necessary. But we cannot simply rebuild Puerto Rico and the U.S. Virgin Islands the way they were. We must go forward to create a strong, sustainable economy and energy system in both territories and address inequities in federal law that have allowed the territories to fall behind in almost every measurable social and economic criteria."

The *Washington Post* called this legislation "an ambitious $146 billion Puerto Rico recovery plan [Sanders] says will allow renewable power sources such as solar and wind to provide about 70 percent of the island's energy needs within the decade. The bill, which has the backing of San Juan Mayor Carmen Yulín Cruz, also calls on Congress to consider retiring Puerto Rico's debt and would give the island billions in additional federal funding for transportation, health care and education in the hopes of stemming a feared mass exodus to the mainland. It would also allocate funds to the Virgin Islands, which were similarly devastated by Hurricane Maria."

THE LOOTING OF THE FEDERAL TREASURY

After failing to pass a "health care" bill that would have thrown as many as 32 million Americans off health insurance, Donald Trump and the Republican leadership did manage to pass their version of "tax reform" in the Senate. Despite a national grassroots campaign in opposition to this giveaway to the rich, the bill passed on December 19 by a strict partisan vote of 51–48. Not one Republican senator voted against it. No Democrat voted for it.

There is no doubt that the tax code is broken and in serious need of reform. For the past forty years, the rich, powerful, and well connected have rigged the tax system to benefit themselves at the expense of the middle class and working families.

But Donald Trump's idea of reforming the tax code was to make a bad situation even worse by giving the wealthiest people and most profitable corporations a huge tax break, while actually increasing taxes on tens of millions of middle-class families.

Of course, that's not how Trump sold his tax plan to the American people. During his campaign for the presidency, Trump repeatedly promised the American people that "the rich will not be gaining at all" from his tax plan and that his bill would provide a "big-league" tax cut for the middle class. He was lying.

According to the nonpartisan Tax Policy Center, by the end of the decade, 83 percent of the tax benefits in Trump's tax plan would go to the top 1 percent. Even more incredibly, the top one-tenth of 1 percent would receive 60 percent of Trump's tax breaks. Meanwhile, 92 million middle-class Americans would actually be paying more in taxes over a ten-year period, including 8 million in the first year alone.

Why is that? Because the tax cuts for middle-class families expire by the end of 2025, while the tax breaks for large corporations would be made permanent. In other words, we have a situation in which the wealthy, who need tax breaks the least, will benefit the most, and many millions of struggling working-class and middle-class families will end up paying more in taxes. How crazy is that?

My Republican colleagues tell the American people that trickle-down economics will expand the economy, create new jobs, and bring in so much revenue that it will magically pay for itself. But the simple truth is that trickle-down economics is a fraudulent theory. It has never worked. When Ronald Reagan slashed taxes for the rich in 1981, economic growth went down by 1.9 percent the following year, and the unemployment rate increased from 7.5 percent to 10.8 percent. The 1981 tax cut was so "successful" that Reagan had to increase taxes eleven times after that.

As the ranking member of the Senate Budget Committee, I have heard Republicans proclaim over and over again how terrible large deficits are and how unfair it is to future generations to leave them with a huge national debt. For my Republican colleagues, deficits are unacceptable when they result from investments in health care, education, affordable housing, or virtually any program that benefits working people. But when it comes to tax breaks for the billionaires and large corporations, deficits are no longer a problem. What hypocrisy!

The Congressional Budget Office has told us that Trump's tax bill would increase the deficit by more than $1.5 trillion over the next decade. And yet not one Republican "deficit hawk" voted against it. By passing this grossly unfair tax reform bill, the Republicans have accomplished two goals very important to them. First, the tax breaks have rewarded their wealthy friends and campaign contributors. Second, by exploding the deficit and national debt, they have laid the groundwork for "balancing the budget" by "shrinking the federal government" through massive cuts to federal programs that benefit the elderly, children, the disabled, the sick, and the poor.

In other words, in an act of extreme cynicism, after giving huge tax breaks to billionaires and large corporations, the Republicans will bemoan the size of the growing deficit and demand cuts to Social Security, Medicare, Medicaid, education, nutrition assistance, affordable housing, and other programs.

What will all this mean for the average American?

It means that after Republicans pass a tax bill that provides a $350,000 tax break to CEOs who make over $10 million a year, they will try to cut Social Security for senior citizens trying to survive on just $12,000 or $13,000 a year.

It means that they will raise the eligibility age for people who are going onto Social Security and Medicare. They will cut the cost-of-living adjustments for senior citizens and disabled veterans. They will slash Medicaid and threaten the nursing home care of millions of seniors.

They will cut Pell grants, making it harder for young people to afford to go to college. They will cut nutrition programs like food stamps and the WIC program, which will make it harder for lower-income Americans to put food on the table. They will cut heating assistance programs so that elderly people will not be able to stay warm in the winter.

No doubt you think I'm exaggerating and that I'm playing partisan politics. I'm not. These are not some wild ideas that I made up. These are concrete proposals that my Republican colleagues have offered time and time again. These are exactly the ideas expressed by Representative Paul Ryan, the Republican Speaker of the House.

In fact, many of these proposals were already included in the budget resolution the Republicans voted for in Congress. They already voted for a $1 trillion cut to Medicaid that would throw 15 million Americans off health insurance. They have already voted to cut Medicare by $500 billion. The Republican chair of the House Ways and Means Subcommittee on Social Security has already introduced legislation that would increase the retirement age and make devastating cuts to Social Security.

Question: Why is it that on issue after issue, the Republicans support legislation strongly opposed by the American people? Why would they want to throw 32 million people off their health insurance when poll after poll shows that idea is wildly unpopular? Why would they implement a tax plan that gives massive tax breaks to billionaires and large corporations, and why would they want to increase the deficit when Americans are opposed? Why do they want to cut Social Security, Medicare, and Medicaid—programs strongly supported by Democrats, Republicans, and Independents alike?

The answer isn't complicated. Follow the money. While this tax legislation is not wanted by the American people, it is wanted by the billionaire class, corporate America, and wealthy campaign contributors. These are the people who have put billions of dollars into the Republican Party and affiliated organizations. This is what they wanted. This is what they paid for. This is payback time.

Representative Chris Collins (R-NY), the first member of Congress to endorse Trump, could not have been blunter about what was at stake when he told a group of reporters, "My donors are basically saying, 'Get it done or don't ever call me again.'" (Collins was later indicted for insider trading.)

Senator Lindsey Graham, a Republican from South Carolina, said, "The financial contributions will stop" if Congress failed to pass Trump's tax plan.

Gary Cohn, Trump's former chief economic adviser, admitted, "The most excited group out there are big CEOs, about our tax plan." In October of 2017, the billionaire Koch brothers network convened a policy summit with one hundred extremely wealthy donors to strategize about how to push their massive tax plan through to the finish line. The headline from a front-page story in the *Boston Globe* says it all: "The Koch Brothers (and Their Friends) Want President Trump's Tax Cut. Very Badly."

The message from the billionaire-led Koch network of donors to President Trump and the Republican Congress it helped to shape couldn't be more clear: Pass a tax overhaul, or else. As the donors mixed and mingled for a policy summit at the St. Regis hotel in midtown Manhattan last week, just a block south from Trump Tower, it came up again. And again. And again. . . . Many in the Koch network, a vast group of libertarian-leaning nonprofits and advocacy and political organizations, described the upcoming legislative push for a tax overhaul as an inflection point in modern political history, a do-or-die moment that would define whether their efforts over the years will pay off or

not. The network leaders plan to dedicate much of their two-
year $400 million politics and policy budget to the effort—
though they wouldn't give an exact number.

Now, $400 million may seem like a lot of money—and it is. But
to the Koch brothers, who are worth over $90 billion, and to their
billionaire friends, spending this kind of money to get tax legislation passed is simply a good investment. The Kochs stood to gain
at least $1 billion a year in tax breaks if this bill were signed into
law. Others in their network would also receive a huge return on
their campaign contribution investment if the Trump tax plan
passed.

Just before final passage, I gave a speech on the Senate floor:

The truth is that what we are seeing today, in an unprecedented
way, is the looting of the Federal Treasury. Today marks a
great victory for the very wealthy campaign contributors
who have contributed hundreds of millions of dollars over
the years to the Republican Party. These billionaires will see a
huge tax break for themselves at the same time as the deficit
of this country is driven up by about $1.5 trillion.

Today is also a victory for the largest and the most profitable
corporations in America, companies such as Apple, Microsoft,
Pfizer, and General Electric, which, despite record-breaking
profits, will now see hundreds of billions of dollars in tax
breaks.

Moving toward passing this very unfair piece of
legislation, the Republican leadership—which controls the
House and the Senate—will move soon to shut down the
Congress and head home for a holiday break. After massive
tax breaks for the rich and large corporations, they believe

their work is done, and they are ready to head home. Well, I respectfully disagree. Maybe, just maybe, before Congress adjourns for the holidays, we should start paying attention to the needs of the working families of this country, to the middle class of this country, and not just the billionaire class.

WE TAKE MEDICARE FOR ALL DIRECTLY TO THE PEOPLE

Political consciousness in the United States is low. Many people don't vote, while many others don't have a clue as to which political party controls the Senate or the House. Most Americans have very little knowledge about the national budget and how their money is spent, the kind of agenda that members of Congress are supporting, or how U.S. economic policies differ from those in other countries.

While many people may not know much about how their government functions, tens of millions do know that they are hurting, and struggling hard to keep their heads above water. Their wages are too low, the cost of housing is too high, and health care and affordable medicine are often inaccessible. And these people ask: Why doesn't anybody in government understand my pain and care about my needs?

One of the great impediments we face as progressives in terms of raising political consciousness and getting people to stand up and fight for their rights is our inability to communicate directly with our constituents about their issues of concern. The truth is that it is very difficult for people to understand what's going on in our country economically or politically, or to imagine an alternative vision, if the corporate media is their major source of information.

Let's be very clear. Corporate media is not "objective"; they are not the "referees" trying to provide "all sides of the story." Corporate media are profit-making entities owned and controlled by the ruling class and some of the wealthiest people in the country. And, like all private corporations, they have an agenda.

To a very significant degree, corporate media sets the terms of our public discourse and what can and cannot be discussed—and those terms are quite limited. They decide what is "important" and what is "not important." As someone who is a frequent guest on mainstream television, I continue to be amazed by how far removed the corporate media is from the struggles of working families. I also never cease to be surprised by how corporate media intentionally avoids the dynamics of wealth and power that shape our nation.

When elected officials are on TV, they're often asked questions about Trump's latest tweet, or about a natural or man-made disaster, or about what is referred to as the "news of the day." While many of these questions might be interesting and important, they very rarely deal with the reality of life that millions of Americans experience.

Today, the top one-tenth of 1 percent owns almost as much wealth as the bottom 90 percent, but I am never asked about the morality of that grotesque inequality, or how the incredible economic power of the few affects governmental decision making. That type of question is beyond the scope of what mainstream media finds acceptable.

I am not asked why it is that for the last forty years the very rich have become much richer, while almost everybody else is getting poorer. I am not asked why it is that, in the wealthiest country in the history of the world, we have the highest rate of childhood poverty of almost any industrialized country on earth, and homelessness is growing at an alarming rate.

I have never been asked why we are the only major country not to guarantee paid family and medical leave, why our people work some of the longest hours of any industrialized country, or why we have more people in jail than any other nation. Despite scientists telling us that climate change is the most serious environmental crisis facing the planet, I am never asked about how we can transform our energy system away from fossil fuel and toward sustainable energy.

Amazingly, I have never been asked about what it means to our country when the extreme Koch brothers, the most powerful political force in America, have, over the years, contributed billions to the Republican Party and a large number of right-wing organizations. There is media interest in how much money they spend, but zero interest in what they stand for. How does that happen?

And, despite my long-term involvement on health care issues, not one mainstream journalist has ever asked me why the United States is the only major country on earth not to guarantee health care for all, and why we spend almost twice as much per capita on health care. Pretty amazing, isn't it? Not if you think about who's paying them hundreds of millions in advertising dollars.

Further, in terms of health care, the power of the insurance companies and the pharmaceutical industry is such that, throughout the entire and endless debate over the Affordable Care Act and every other recent piece of legislation on health care, there has not been one congressional hearing about a simpler, more cost-effective, and more popular approach: Medicare for All. Medicare is the most popular health insurance program in the country, and recent polls suggest that a strong majority of Americans support Medicare for All.

Nonetheless, Medicare for All is not an issue to be discussed in Congress. Medicare for All is not an issue to be discussed in the media.

Well, I intended to change that.

That is why I decided to put together the first U.S. Senate-sponsored town hall meeting on Medicare for All in American history. I wanted to bring experts together for a thorough discussion of the nature of our current dysfunctional system and how we could provide health care for every man, woman, and child in our country at a far lower cost.

As part of that discussion, I also wanted to focus on how our current, very expensive system affected the business community in terms of international competitiveness. What did it mean for American businesses to have to compete against companies in other countries where all the employees had government-paid-for health care? What did it mean for company productivity when some employees were on the job not because they wanted to be there or because they enjoyed the work but because they needed the health insurance? What did it mean for the future of our economy when health care costs were now nearly 18 percent of our GDP?

Lastly, I thought it would be important to see how the health care system in the United States compared with what other countries were doing. For years, we had been told by my Republican colleagues that our system was the best in the world. We were told over and over again about all the problems that national health systems abroad had. Was that true? What was the patient and doctor experience in other countries where the cost of patient treatment was not an issue? What did it mean to people abroad who could go to the doctor whenever they wanted, without worrying about out-of-pocket expenses? How was health care affected when prescription drugs were free or inexpensive? Were people in countries around the world revolting against their national health care systems and clamoring for an American-style approach?

While a town hall meeting on Medicare for All was a great idea, it wouldn't mean much if there weren't a significant viewing audience. How could we hold a town hall that reached millions of people? I suggested the idea to an anchor at one of the major networks. He said he would get back to me. I'm still waiting for the call.

It then occurred to my staff and me that we had to go outside the box and do something revolutionary. We knew the mainstream media was not going to produce a town hall meeting on a concept that was vehemently opposed by the insurance and drug companies. It just wasn't going to happen. That was the bad news.

The good news was that television viewing in America was undergoing radical change. Fewer people were getting their news and programming from the traditional networks. More people, especially young people, were now getting their information and entertainment online. This was something my office well understood. We had used such platforms as Facebook Live and Instagram, and other approaches, to communicate with our audience on many occasions, and with success.

The challenge we now faced was whether we could produce a high-quality ninety-minute town hall meeting online, something far more complicated than anything we had done previously. We were not CNN or CBS. We were a U.S. Senate office. Did we have the capability of producing a town hall meeting that was not only informative but technically proficient, and interesting enough to hold the attention of a large viewing audience? Further, could we get some of the leading progressive digital media companies to coproduce the program with us, lending us their expertise? And finally, at a time when we were told that the American people had a short attention span, would anyone watch a long, wonky program about a complicated issue?

On the night of January 23, 2018, we got our answer. The town hall meeting was broadcast from the beautiful auditorium at the Visitor Center of the U.S. Capitol before a standing-room-only audience of more than 450 people. It was streamed online not only by my office's Facebook page but by such leading progressive digital operations as the Young Turks, ATTN:, and NowThis News. Numerous progressive groups and individuals, including MoveOn, CREDO Action, the PCCC, and Robert Reich, shared our broadcast with their audiences. I was also grateful to many of my Senate colleagues who support Medicare for All, who helped us promote the event on their social media.

The format was pretty straightforward. We had three panels. First, we described the dysfunctionality of the current system. Second, we talked about the positive impact that Medicare for All would have on the business community. Third, we took a look at what universal health care meant in countries around the world.

The first panel included Stan Brock, the founder of Remote Area Medical, the largest nongovernmental provider of free mobile medical clinics in the United States. Stan described how, in the richest country in the world, his organization has had to provide free medical, dental, and vision care to nearly 1 million Americans in some of the poorest parts of the country, people forced to sleep in their cars and makeshift tents for days at a time, as they awaited care from Stan's volunteer medical team.

The panel also included Dr. Claudia Fegan, chief medical officer for the Cook County Health and Hospitals System, which serves more than 1 million visitors a year in the Chicago area. Dr. Fegan told us that 36,000 people died in 2016 in this country alone as a result of having no insurance. She gave some examples of what life is like when you can't afford health care, including the copayments: the fifty-six-year-old cook with hypertension but no medication who had a stroke on the way home from work; the sixty-four-year-old salesman, also with hypertension, who thought he could tough it out until he was sixty-five and could get Medicare, but who developed kidney problems and now needed dialysis; and the fifty-four-year-old nurse's aide who came in with difficulty swallowing and was found to have advanced esophageal cancer. She wanted to schedule her radiation treatments at certain times of day so she could still work and pay the bills, because nothing else mattered. Dr. Fegan emphasized that we need to make health care a right in this country, that we allow too many people who aren't involved in the delivery of health care to profit from it, and that it would be much more cost-effective to take care of people earlier on while alleviating considerable—and unnecessary—suffering.

Deborah Wachtel, a nurse practitioner, was also on the panel. She discussed how the high cost of prescription drugs affects her patients and how much time she spends arguing with insurance companies, each of which has a different set of rules for approving a prescription.

The second panel included Richard Master, the founder and CEO of MCS Industries Inc., a $200 million-a-year company. Master is tired of spending huge amounts of money on health care for his employees in a system that is incredibly wasteful and bureaucratic, and he expressed his view that the best way to ensure the competitiveness of American business is with a Medicare for All, single-payer health care system.

Jen Kimmich was also on the business panel. She cofounded the Alchemist brewery in 2003 and advocates for Medicare for All because, as a business leader, she believes that when her employees and their families are healthy, and guaranteed health care is a right, her business does better.

The third panelist was Dr. Don Berwick, a pediatrician who, in the Obama administration, served as director of the Centers for Medicare and Medicaid Services. As former head of the Medicare program, he expressed his view that Medicare for All is the best system in terms of transparency, patient engagement, quality improvement, and patient safety. He told the audience, "You can stand up for people" when you have a single-payer health care system serving a large number of Americans. "Why wouldn't we do that for all Americans, not just people over sixty-five?"

The third panel consisted of a doctor from Canada, a doctor from Norway, and a young American who had worked in France.

Dr. Danyaal Raza is a family doctor in downtown Toronto. He expressed his strong support for the Canadian single-payer system because he believes doctors should be able to provide the treatment patients need regardless of their financial situation. He contrasted how he is able to provide care with what he has heard from some of his American colleagues.

Dr. Meetali Kakad is a public health physician in Oslo. She made a point that Dr. Raza had also made: that the universal health care system in her country has support all across the political spectrum, and that politicians would not win election if they did not believe that health care was a right, not a privilege.

Jill Tipton, a young person from Wisconsin who had studied and worked in France, was also on the third panel. She noted how complicated and time-consuming it was navigating the U.S. system, and how much easier and less expensive it was getting health care through the French national health care system.

The town hall meeting was wonky, deeply "in the weeds" at

times, and long—it lasted the full ninety minutes we'd planned for it to go. It also included prerecorded video questions and live questions from the audience.

Was it a success?

The meeting received a fair amount of media coverage but its reception was captured best, I believe, in an article by Theo Anderson for *In These Times*, a progressive weekly paper, entitled "Bernie Sanders Just Sidestepped Corporate Media to Promote Medicare for All to 1 Million Viewers." Its lede said it all: "The revolution will not be televised, but it might be live-streamed."

Anderson elaborated:

> *The Medicare for All town hall may have been but a small step, yet it confirmed that Sanders—who has about 7.5 million Facebook followers, hosts a podcast, and regularly creates polished and shareable video content—recognizes the promise of the burgeoning new media infrastructure and is moving quickly to take advantage of it. Which is a wise move if you say you want a revolution. [Young Turks Network] has nearly 3.6 million YouTube subscribers. ATTN: has nearly 5.6 million Facebook followers. NowThis has about 13 million Facebook followers.*

And he concluded:

> *In order to achieve these radical policy changes, Sanders has made it a priority to educate Americans on both the profound challenges we face and how we can take them on. He has shown a stubborn belief that the people, supplied with the true facts of the situation, will choose to build a better democracy. And, consequently, detailed discussion of policy actually matters. In*

spite of everything we have learned about the state of the nation recently, a live-streamed town hall on health care policy is "a little bit revolutionary." And a cause for hope.

As I said to Young Turks host Ana Kasparian that night, my hope was that our Medicare for All town hall meeting would prove to be the first step in bringing millions of people into a serious discussion about one of the major issues facing our country.

THE BIGGEST CHALLENGE

On January 31, my friend and fellow Vermonter Bill McKibben, the writer, climate activist, and founder of 350.org, invited me to participate in an important event at George Washington University. Along with the Reverend Lennox Yearwood Jr., head of the Hip Hop Caucus and the Howard University Gospel Choir, we were there to talk about climate change.

In the audience and watching on a livestream were thousands of students, black, white, Latino, Native American, and Asian American, brought together as part of the Fossil Free campaign. These young people are standing up and demanding that their elected leaders, from mayors to Congress, move toward a 100 percent renewable energy economy and away from fossil fuels. In many ways, they are leading the effort to save our planet, and I was proud and inspired to be with them.

I delayed flying back to Vermont to participate in this event because I wanted these young people to know that they had my strong support for the work they were doing on their campuses and in their communities. They understood the sad reality that the current political leadership in this country and around much of the world has failed them on this life-and-death issue and that, if the planet were going to be saved, they would have to lead the fight.

Among many international organizations being led by young people demanding that we find the courage to take on the fossil fuel industry, 350.org is working to transform our energy system away from fossil fuels and into energy efficiency and sustainable energy. The time is late, and they want action *now*.

In my view, given the extraordinary wealth and power of the oil, gas, and coal companies and the general cowardice of politicians to oppose them, the activism of these students is one of the major forces that has the potential to save this planet from the calamity that will occur if we continue along the present course.

In my remarks to these young people, I said:

I am truly inspired by the work that you are doing. While Donald Trump and his friends want to divide us up, you are helping to bring people from all walks of life together. You are doing that not only here in the United States but all over the world because when we talk about climate change, you know and I know that we are talking about a global crisis and that it is imperative that we bring people from all over the world together to fight to save this planet.

Last night, we heard President Trump's State of the Union address. And it is my job as a United States senator to have to be there. It's what I have to do. But among the many other absurd and dishonest and ugly things that he said, there is one interesting reality. If you go to the scientific community and ask them what the major global crisis we face is, the vast majority of them will say it is climate change. And they will say that it is absolutely imperative that we reduce carbon emissions by transforming our energy system away from fossil fuel to sustainable energy. And yet, Donald Trump spoke last night for over an hour, he talked about many things, but somehow, he forgot to mention the words "climate change." What an outrage!

But we should not be surprised because Donald Trump, one of the great "scientists" of our time, has determined after years and years of exhaustive study that climate change is a hoax brought to us from China.

It is hard to keep track of the outrageous and destructive behavior of Donald Trump. However, the greatest long-term threat caused by his administration is that not only is it failing to take action to stop climate change, but it is actually taking steps to make the problem worse. The tragic and undisputed truth is that the Trump administration rejects science, ignores the reality of climate change, and pursues policies that are directly leading to more carbon emissions and a major exacerbation of the crisis. On behalf of its friends in the fossil fuel industry, the administration is doing exactly the opposite of what must be done.

In 2017, federal scientists announced that the string of the four warmest years on record across the globe continued. According to the NOAA, in 2017, the average temperature across global land and ocean surfaces was 1.51 degrees Fahrenheit (0.84 degrees Celsius) above the twentieth-century average. This was the third-highest temperature since 1880, behind 2016 (the warmest) and 2015 (the second warmest).

When I traveled to Florida to campaign for gubernatorial candidate Andrew Gillum in August 2018, I ran right into the horror of what climate change is doing. While I was there, the Florida media was full of stories about how the state was confronting a "toxic algae" crisis. These toxic outbreaks, exacerbated by climate change, were destroying the state's beaches, threatening the tourism that fuels Florida's economy, and driving hundreds of residents into hospitals because of respiratory illnesses. Further, the Gillum campaign staff who drove me around that day told me about roads in South Florida that were flooded, even at low tide, because the sea was rising. Scientists predict, in fact, that if we continue down the path we are on, much of coastal Florida, including Miami, will be underwater by the end of the century.

But it's not, of course, just Florida. We are facing a national and planetary crisis. In August 2018, as a result of the heat and dryness, California experienced its worst forest fire season in history, with over one million acres burned.

Unbelievably, at exactly the same time that California was burning and toxic algae was causing panic in Florida, Donald Trump announced a series of measures that would increase carbon emissions—including abandoning long-term fuel economy standards for passenger cars and light trucks developed by the Obama administration.

In the midst of the many reckless policy decisions made by the Trump administration, as well as the day-to-day revelations from the Mueller investigation, Stormy Daniels, Omarosa, Paul Manafort, Michael Cohen, and so on, it is easy to forget about what this administration is doing to our environment. The truth is, however, that Trump's refusal to acknowledge the reality of climate change and to help us move away from fossil fuels will not only adversely affect our generation, but it will make this planet far less healthy and habitable for our kids, grandchildren, and future generations. To sacrifice the future of the planet for the short-term profits of the fossil fuel industry is unspeakably selfish, outrageous, and unforgivable.

I am convinced that the crisis of climate change gets far too little attention. On August 17, 2018, I recorded a short video discussing Trump's war against our planet. It was viewed by over 1.5 million people. This is what I said:

In case you haven't noticed, it's hot outside. It's hot throughout the United States, it's hot throughout Europe, it's hot throughout much of the world. In fact, the last five years have been the warmest years on record and scientists tell us that if we do not take aggressive action in lowering carbon emissions, it's going to get worse—much worse.

California is now experiencing the worst wildfires in their history. Glacier—yes, Glacier—National Park is on fire. Greece is expecting its hottest year on record, and fast-moving fires have killed at least ninety people. Sweden struggled to contain more than fifty fires amidst its worst drought in seventy-four years. A heat wave in eastern Canada has been blamed for at least seventy deaths.

And that is just some of what's going on right now.

It is true that Donald Trump gave over a trillion dollars in tax breaks to the top 1 percent, while he is proposing massive cuts to Medicare, Medicaid, and the Social Security disability fund. It is true that Trump wanted to throw 32 million Americans off the health care they have. And it's true that Trump is working overtime to divide us up by the color of our skin, gender, sexual orientation, religion, and country of origin.

All of that is terrible, to say the least. But what might be even worse is that President Trump and his friends in the fossil fuel industry, in the name of short-term profits, are destroying the planet that we will be leaving our children and grandchildren.

We cannot allow this to continue. I urge all of you to stand up, fight back, and get active in the political process.

If we are bold, if we have the courage to take on the fossil fuel industry, if we are prepared to invest in sustainable energy, we can make the necessary changes to save the planet. And that's exactly what we have to do.

AN UGLY DAY IN THE SENATE

Today, two amendments designed to provide legal protections and a path to citizenship for 1.8 million Dreamers were defeated in the Senate. They both got over 50 votes but needed 60. We were able to get only eight Republicans to vote with us. It was an ugly day, with the strong odor of xenophobia and racism in the air.

There are some 800,000 immigrants in the Deferred Action for Childhood Arrivals (DACA) program, and another million who are eligible for the program. These are young people who were brought into this country by their parents illegally, often as infants, but who have spent virtually their entire lives here in the United States. Almost all of these young people are working, or in school, or in the military. I was impressed to learn that some 20,000 of them are teachers.

Over the past two years, I have had the opportunity to meet with Dreamers on a number of occasions. Several of them, in fact, worked in my presidential campaign and did a great job. A few days before the vote, I had a number of Dreamers in my office. They talked about their concerns not only for themselves but for their parents, who had worked so hard to support and educate them. They also expressed what DACA meant to them in terms of being able to legally hold down a job, go to school, or simply drive a car without fear. They are proud of this country. They want to become citizens.

The DACA issue poses a great moral crisis for this country. Can we turn our backs on these 1.8 million young people, allow them to lose their legal status and be subject to deportation—to be thrown out of the only country they have ever known? If that were to happen, it would be a moral stain on this country that would never be forgotten.

As the son of an immigrant, who came to this country with limited education and skills and who might have been denied entrance to Trump's America, I feel very strongly about this issue. The day before the vote, I was on the Senate floor. I stated, "Mr. President, this whole debate over immigration and the Dreamers has become somewhat personal for me, because it has reminded me that I am a first-generation American, the son of an immigrant who came to this country at the age of seventeen without a nickel in his pocket, a high school dropout who knew no English and had no particular trade."

I continued: "But the truth is that immigration is not just my story. It's not just the story of my wife's family who came from Ireland. It is the story of America, and of tens of millions of families who came from every single part of this world."

Amazingly, poll after poll shows that a very strong majority of Americans—Democrats, Republicans, and Independents—want to protect the Dreamers. Some of the polls have support for the Dreamers at over 80 percent. We can't get 80 percent of the American people to agree on their favorite ice cream, but they are united in support of these young people.

Yet, despite overwhelming public support, we still couldn't get legislation passed to protect them. On the day of the vote, Trump weighed in heavily against the amendments, and his Department of Homeland Security sent out an unprecedented hysterical and xenophobic statement grossly distorting what the amendments would do. Sadly, Mitch McConnell and the Republican leadership paid more attention to their extremist xenophobic supporters than to what the American people want. It was a bitter loss.

The immigration system in this country is acknowledged by almost everyone to be a disaster. It has not been overhauled for thirty years. And it is not just DACA. Millions of undocumented people have been in this country for decades, living in the shadows, fearful that on any given day they could be arrested and deported, while nonetheless working hard, raising families, and, according to *Forbes*, paying more than $11.5 billion in state and local taxes.

In 2008, I visited with tomato workers in Immokalee, Florida, to help them raise wages and improve the deplorable living and working conditions they experienced. With a wink and a nod, everyone in the community knew that most of these workers were undocumented. But everyone also knew there would be no tomato industry there without them. That's also true in my own state of Vermont, where some 1,000 undocumented people, mostly from Mexico, work on dairy farms. Without these workers, the dairy industry in Vermont would be in desperate shape.

The truth is that American agriculture is heavily dependent upon undocumented immigrants. In fact, it is estimated that about half of the agricultural workers in this country are undocumented. Instead of demagoguing this issue, we need to pass comprehensive immigration reform and provide a path toward citizenship. In 2013, that is what the U.S. Senate did. Unfortunately, that bill went nowhere in the Republican House of Representatives.

MORE CHILDREN KILLED BY GUNS

There are eight rooms in my Senate office complex in DC, and the TV is always on in some of them. I was in the office of my scheduler, Jake Gillison, when the dreaded words appeared across the bottom of his TV screen. "School Shooting in Parkland, Florida. Fatalities Feared." By the time all the information was in, we learned that seventeen people had been killed in another school shooting— fourteen students and three adults, with fourteen wounded.

Four months after the slaughter outside a Las Vegas hotel, when fifty-eight people were killed and five hundred wounded, Americans all across the country were asking, "When will it end? Will gun violence and mass shootings in this country ever stop? What can we do?"

The day after the Parkland shooting, I attended a play at a Burlington elementary school that my grandson was in. Before the play began, the principal of the school made the usual introductory and welcoming remarks. But he also seemed to put a strong emphasis on pointing out the exits in the auditorium—what to do in an emergency. In the back of his mind, was he worried about the possibility of a gun disaster happening that evening? Was that what millions of parents were thinking about when they now sent their kids off to school? And what kind of terrible fears now existed in the minds of eight-year-olds who no longer felt safe in their classrooms? How would these mass slaughters affect their whole lives? What kind of insane world were we living in?

Nobody has any simple or magical answers to the question of how we end mass shootings or the widespread gun violence we experience. The television, movie, and video game industries make billions out of showing an incredible amount of ugly and gratuitous violence, normalizing it. There are hundreds of millions of guns floating around this country, including some 5 million military-style assault weapons designed solely to kill human beings. In a nation facing a severe mental health crisis, where life expectancy is in decline because of alcoholism, drug addiction, and suicide, there are thousands of people walking the streets in every state in the country at their wits' end—suicidal and/or homicidal, with no place to turn. We are a nation with a dysfunctional health care system and have nowhere near the mental health treatment capabilities we need.

Shortly after the mass shooting that killed their friends and teachers, some brave students from Marjory Stoneman Douglas High School in Parkland came together to demand that government finally take action to prevent further shootings. Instead of simply grieving the loss of their fellow students, they decided to stand up and fight back. They wondered, as we all wonder, how a nineteen-year-old youngster who was known to be at risk for violence could have legally purchased at least ten guns, including a variant of an AK-47, the assault weapon he allegedly used. How could it be that in Florida it is easier to buy an assault weapon than it is to register to vote?

While there may not be any guaranteed answers as to how we end mass shootings, that does not mean we should not be doing everything possible to prevent them. These murders not only cost us innocent lives—in Parkland, Las Vegas, Orlando, Virginia Tech, Sandy Hook, and so many other locations—but they also impact the fiber of our nation and sap the energy, hope, and optimism of our people. What kind of country are we when, time after time, sick people walk into schools and shoot down innocent children?

While this crisis will not be easily solved, despair and inactivity are not options. We need action. And the good news is that while the American people are divided over various aspects of gun control, the more important truth is that there is now widespread and growing agreement on a variety of actions that would almost certainly lower the level of gun violence in this country.

An October 12, 2017, Quinnipiac University national poll found that:

American voters support, by 94 percent to 5 percent, requiring background checks for all gun purchases. Voters in gun-owning households support universal background checks 93 percent to 6 percent.

Support for other nationwide gun measures is:

- 79–19 percent for a mandatory waiting period for all gun purchases;
- 64–32 percent for a ban on the sale of assault weapons;
- 86–12 percent for a ban on the sale of guns to people convicted of a violent crime;
- 58–38 percent for stricter regulations on ammunition sales;

- 64–34 percent for a ban on high-capacity magazines that hold more than ten rounds.

American voters say, 63–27 percent, that it's possible to make new gun laws without interfering with gun rights. Republican voters say, 51–37 percent, that it's possible to make gun laws that don't interfere with gun rights, and voters in gun households agree, 57–33 percent.

Other polls show similar results. In other words, by large numbers, the American people support commonsense gun safety legislation. Why, then, aren't we going forward? The answer, sadly, is that Congress is not listening to the American people on this issue. They are listening to the very well-funded NRA, an organization with enormous political power. The NRA has long ceased being a gun rights advocacy group. It is now an integral and powerful part of the Republican Party infrastructure. Trust me. When the NRA speaks, the Republican members of Congress listen, big time.

I was invited to appear on *Meet the Press* on February 18, a few days after the shooting in Parkland. The host, Chuck Todd, and I discussed gun issues. This is what I said:

Chuck, what I just told you is that for thirty years, I believe that we should not be selling assault weapons in this country. These weapons are not for hunting, they are for killing human beings. These are military weapons. I do not know why we have five million of them running around the United States of America, so of course we have to do that. Of course we have to make it harder for people to purchase weapons. We have people now who are on terrorist watch lists who can purchase a weapon. Does this make any sense to anybody? Bottom line here, Republicans are going to have to say that it's more important to protect the children of this country than to antagonize the NRA. Are they prepared to do that? I surely hope they are.

And let me repeat that. The time is long overdue for the Republicans in Congress to stand up to the NRA and protect the children of this country.

ON THE ROAD AGAIN

At the end of the day, the best way to change minds, activate people, and win elections is to communicate with your constituents face-to-face. I fully understand that TV and radio ads play an important role in political campaigns, as does social media, but the most effective tool that we have for serious politics is getting out and directly communicating with the people. It's also a lot of fun.

Face-to-face politics can take place by knocking on doors or by walking down Main Street and engaging people. It can happen through town hall meetings. It can happen by marching in parades. It can happen by holding large rallies. As a candidate, I have done all of that and much more—and I love doing it.

I often get amused by my colleagues in Congress and the pundits on television who keep asking, "How can we turn Trump's working-class supporters around? How can we make them understand that Trump's agenda is for billionaires, not for them?" Well, here is a wild and crazy idea not very often acted upon. Why don't we go out and respectfully talk to them in the communities in which they live?

And that's what I did on the weekend of February 23, with well-attended rallies in Illinois, Iowa, Wisconsin, and Michigan. Some of the rallies were cosponsored by Not One Penny, a progressive organization opposed to Trump's tax giveaways to the rich. Other rallies were cosponsored by progressive candidates.

Our first rally was in Chicago, which is definitely not Trump country. It is, however, the home of the Chicago Democratic Party machine, a powerful political organization. Over the years, Chuy García has become a good friend of mine. He is a progressive member of the Cook County Board of Commissioners and a leader in the Illinois Latino community. Now he was running for Congress in a seat vacated by Luis Gutiérrez.

Several years ago, Chuy ran a brilliant and surprisingly effective campaign for mayor against Rahm Emanuel, the machine-backed and well-funded Democrat. In that campaign, he did exactly what progressives have to do. He put together a strong grassroots working-class coalition of whites, blacks, Latinos, and young people.

During his campaign for mayor, I attended a rally for Chuy at a union hall on Chicago's South Side. It was a great meeting, standing room only, enormous energy. Chuy ended up losing the race in a runoff election, but Sue Sadlowski Garza, a political ally of his and a candidate for the board of aldermen, won, in an upset victory. I was happy to have helped her. During my campaign for president, Chuy more than reciprocated the support I had given him. He was at my side time and again as we traveled the country, and he played an especially important role in Illinois, where we almost pulled off a major upset against Clinton.

Now I was back in Chicago for his campaign for Congress. It was another great event. A mariachi band; a beautiful theater and a packed house with a diverse audience (different ages, different colors, different backgrounds); and a rousing introductory speech by Nina Turner, the president of Our Revolution.

What I liked most about Chuy's campaign was that he was in it not just for himself. He was actively supporting a number of young Latino and black candidates who were taking on the Democratic machine in Chicago at various levels. There is nothing more inspiring than seeing bright young people getting involved in politics, and that's what Chuy was helping to make happen. As we left Chicago, I promised to help not only Chuy but these young candidates as well. And then it was on to Iowa.

I love Iowa. It is a small rural state like my own state of Vermont, with down-to-earth, hardworking people. Today it is a state strongly controlled by the Republican Party. Its two senators are Republican. Its governor is Republican. Its state legislature is Republican. In my view, it is a state not so much won by Republicans as lost by Democrats, who have not been bold enough in standing up for the working people of that state. I was in Iowa to try to change that, by supporting a candidate who was fighting for a progressive agenda, a candidate who would provide a real choice for voters.

Iowa, of course, holds the first nominating contest in the presidential primary process. As a result, in 2015, I spent a lot of time in Iowa and got to know many of the people there. In fact, we ended up doing over one hundred town hall meetings and rallies in every nook and cranny of the state. The person who helped coordinate that successful campaign for me was Pete D'Alessandro, and he was now running for Congress. Like Chuy García, Pete is from the working class and has not forgotten where he came from.

The rally for Pete in Des Moines was spirited and, for a Friday afternoon, well attended. A few days after the event, we were able to send out a fund-raising request for Pete that brought in a significant number of small donations for his campaign. In the evening, we did a large rally with Not One Penny, in Cedar Rapids, Iowa. In a state controlled by Republicans and won by Trump, there was still significant grassroots energy against his tax proposal.

And now it was on to Wisconsin—another state that, in recent years, has drifted far to the right under Republican rule, but a state that I had won during the primary process. As the progressive publication *Mother Jones* stated, "In Wisconsin, the senator is fomenting a working-class Rust Belt insurrection against Trump." They got that right. That's exactly what I was doing.

The major event of the day was a rally in Racine, with Randy Bryce, a union ironworker who, at the time of the rally, was taking on the most powerful Republican in Congress, House Speaker Paul Ryan.

It is fair to say that there was no House race more important than this, and that the eyes of the nation were on District 1, Wisconsin. I was delighted to be in Racine with Randy, because the competing ideologies that were reflected in this campaign reflect the different visions of where our country should be heading. On one side was a candidate who was addressing the needs of working families. On the other side was a candidate who was supporting the greed of the billionaire class.

Paul Ryan is the flesh-and-blood representative of oligarchy. He is fully supported by the Koch brothers, the third-richest family in America, and other billionaires. According to the *Washington Examiner*, "House Speaker Paul Ryan collected nearly $500,000 in campaign contributions from Charles Koch and his wife after helping usher through a massive tax reform law. According to a recent campaign finance report filed Thursday, Koch and his wife, Elizabeth, each donated $247,700 to Ryan's joint fund-raising committee. Five other donors, including billionaire businessmen Jeffery Hildebrand and William Parfet, each contributed $100,000 in the last quarter of 2017, according to the records, which were first reported by the *International Business Times*."

But it's not just the Koch brothers and the wealthiest individuals in the country. Paul Ryan is strongly supported by Wall Street, the fossil fuel industry, the pharmaceutical industry, the military-industrial complex, and all of the powerful special interests that dominate the economic and political life of our country. At that moment, he had an astounding $10 million in his campaign coffers, but even that number is misleading. Given his unqualified support from corporate America and the 1 percent, there was no limit to the amount of money he and his supporters could raise for his reelection.

There is a reason why the billionaire class loves Ryan, and that is because his ideology is that of a right-wing extremist. He worked hard to repeal the Affordable Care Act and supported efforts to throw as many as 32 million Americans off the health insurance they currently have. He helped write the Republican tax bill, which provides massive tax breaks to corporate America and provides, at the end of ten years, 83 percent of its benefits to the top 1 percent. He has been one of the most aggressive members of Congress in trying to cut and privatize Social Security, Medicare, and Medicaid. There is virtually no federal program that benefits working families, the elderly, children, or the sick that Ryan would not cut.

Randy Bryce is a candidate with a radically different vision from Ryan's, and he comes from an entirely different world than Ryan's. A year before he announced his candidacy, he was employed as an ironworker and, during his work career, had suffered many of the same problems as other people in the district, including unemployment and poverty. He is exactly the kind of candidate that the Democratic Party needs to attract.

Randy's agenda is the agenda of the working class of America. He wants to raise the minimum wage to $15 an hour and create millions of well-paying jobs by rebuilding our crumbling infrastructure. He demands that the rich start paying their fair share of taxes. He wants to make public colleges and universities tuition-free, and he believes that health care for all is a right, not a privilege.

The turnout for the rally was extraordinary. On a Saturday afternoon in Racine, we brought out over 2,000 people. There was not an empty seat in the auditorium, and the overflow section was packed as well. It was especially exciting to look out at the crowd and see the front rows filled by members of the United Automobile Workers (UAW) and other unions. They were there to support one of their own.

As a local TV station reported, "The crowd roared as Sanders took the stage Saturday at Memorial Hall in Racine. 'We need to get rid of Republican control over the House and of the Senate and bring in leadership that is prepared to fight for working people, not just billionaires,' Sanders said."

What I also said is that the political revolution is alive and growing. More and more Americans, in Wisconsin and across the country, are beginning to stand up and fight for a government that represents all of us and not just the powerful few. The event with Randy was powerful and moving.

Can a candidate like Randy Bryce, an ordinary working person, defeat one of the most powerful and well-funded politicians in the country? We will never know, because Paul Ryan chose not to defend his seat instead of facing a tough reelection fight. But having seen the size and enthusiasm of that crowd in Racine, I wouldn't have bet against Randy.

In the evening, we headed to Green Bay, a conservative part of Wisconsin that had voted for Trump. On the drive in, we stopped at Lambeau Field and recorded a video in front of the statue of Vince Lombardi. To their enormous credit, the people of Green Bay are the only community in the country with a publicly owned NFL team.

Once again, the crowd at the Not One Penny rally was large. Here, my attack against the president was not just about his dishonesty and his reactionary economic policies. It was also about his cynical effort to divide the nation. I said that Trump was "try[ing] to divide the American people. You have presidents who have been conservative, liberal, and progressive. But every president has understood that when you get to the Oval Office, your job is to bring our people together. Now, for cheap political reasons, what we're seeing is a president who is dividing us up, a president who is pushing racism and sexism and xenophobia. . . . This country has struggled for too long fighting bigotry. We're not going backward. We're going forward."

Our last public event was in Lansing, Michigan, a state that Trump won by less than 1 percent. Once again, the turnout was strong, over 2,000. One of the major points that I made in Lansing was that as a result of our strong showing in 2016, including our victory in Michigan, many of the "radical" ideas that we had proposed during the campaign were now being seriously discussed throughout the country and, in some cases, being adopted. As the *Detroit News* reported:

> *Sanders opened his speech by recounting his 2016 campaign, including his surprise Michigan primary victory over eventual*

Democratic nominee Hillary Clinton. The self-described
Democratic socialist said many of his ideas once criticized as too
"radical" or "extreme" have become part of the mainstream
debate, including his calls for tuition-free college, a "Medicare
for all" single-payer health system and a $15 minimum wage.

He urged supporters to continue those fights. "You can have
great candidates, you can have great ideas, but unless you have
a movement of people behind those ideas, we will not succeed,"
he said.

After the rally in Lansing, we drove to Flint, Michigan, for a closed-door meeting with Pastor Ezra Tillman Jr. and local residents at the First Trinity Missionary Baptist Church. Most Americans know that Flint is the city where the residents, including many children, were poisoned by high levels of lead in the drinking water. It is also a very poor city, with a majority African American population. During my campaign for president, I visited Flint twice, in one case holding a town hall meeting, and I promised that I would return after the election whether I won or lost. I kept my promise.

All the meetings I have held in Flint have been painful and emotional. This is a city under siege, with enormous problems, where the residents feel ignored and betrayed. Imagine, in a closed room, hearing from a mother whose daughter had been a bright, gregarious young girl and then, as a result of exposure to lead in the water, suffered neurological damage that significantly limited her cognitive and emotional abilities. Then understand that she was just one of many casualties.

While having the most toxic water system in the country, the residents of Flint were forced to pay the highest water bills in America—and they're still paying them. How is that for powerlessness: paying outrageous prices for a basic necessity that, because of government malfunction, is causing brain damage and destroying lives?

Meetings like these are extremely difficult for me. The problems in Flint—a poisonous water system, poverty, racism, high unemployment, poor schools, and inadequate health care—are not going to be easily solved within the current political and economic framework of Michigan or the United States. In Washington, Congress is much too busy working on tax breaks for billionaires to worry about the people of Flint. While the very rich get much richer, the people of Flint continue to be ignored and continue to suffer.

In the midst of all that, what could I honestly say to the people in the room? What kind of legitimate hope could I offer them? What they don't need are more lies and promises that will not be kept.

Amidst all of these problems, however, I would be remiss not to point out the incredible dignity, intelligence, and resiliency of the people we met with. They inspired me deeply. I saw more humanity in a one-hour meeting there than I see in a year in Congress. I was especially impressed by the beautiful high school students who were there, black and white. They are not giving up. As best they can, they are fighting back for their community and their future.

The one promise that I made at that meeting was that I would not forget Flint. We would work with the people there in any and every way possible.

POLITICS AND BASEBALL

I have never believed the pundits who talk about "red states" and "blue states." Never accepted it—just not my experience. On the contrary, I have always believed that so long as there are working people who are struggling, so long as there are candidates who have the guts to take on big money and speak to the realities facing the working class, those candidates can win—anywhere.

This "red state" mythology is a self-fulfilling prophecy. Democrats think they can't win in particular states, they don't put resources into those states, and, shock of all shocks, they lose in those states. Tragically, this is true even in some of the poorest states in the country, where working people are suffering terribly under right-wing Republican rule.

One of my goals over the last several years has been to help create a fifty-state Democratic Party. It is beyond comprehension that Democrats have essentially conceded half the states in this country to Republicans. As part of that effort, I have traveled to many red states, including those that Trump won by big margins. Since the 2016 election, I have been to Montana, Mississippi, Kansas,

West Virginia, Kentucky, Pennsylvania, Ohio, Indiana, Georgia, Florida, Iowa, Wisconsin, Nebraska, and Utah. In virtually all of those states, we have held great rallies, with large turnouts.

On the weekend of March 9, 2018, we visited two more red states, Texas and Arizona. It was a fascinating trip.

In Texas, we did rallies in San Antonio and Lubbock that were organized by Our Revolution. Nina Turner, who had taken over the presidency of Our Revolution from Jeff Weaver and was doing a great job, traveled with us and introduced me at the events. We were accompanied by my old friend and longtime progressive Jim Hightower, who has been active in Texas politics for decades.

In San Antonio, as we walked through that very beautiful city, I found myself doing a lot of selfies and handshaking. I was impressed by the strong support we received out on the streets, especially from the Latino community. The rally we did that evening was no different. The Laurie Auditorium on the Trinity University campus was filled, bursting with energy from a beautifully diverse crowd, especially students. The *San Antonio Current* quoted one who captured the scene perfectly: "'We've already talked to people who were going to sneak in because they ran out of free tickets,' said Brian Callanan, 33, who drove down from Austin with his partner Erika Aurioles, 27, to hear the progressive firebrand and 2016 presidential contender. 'I mean, look around: there are college students, there are old people, there are working people.'"

The event in San Antonio was fun and exciting. The event in Lubbock, however, was more important in that it told me everything I needed to know about the ineptitude of the Democratic Party and why Donald Trump was president. Texas is a supposedly conservative state, and Lubbock is one of the most conservative parts of Texas—which is precisely why we went there, at Jim's suggestion. And what happened is that in this supposedly conservative area, we had a large, standing-room-only rally with enormous enthusiasm. The *Lubbock Avalanche-Journal* reported, "Progressives on the Panhandle/South Plains hadn't had a political rally like what took place Saturday afternoon at the Lubbock Memorial Civic Center in a long time, if ever."

Here is what is interesting about that.

The population of Lubbock County is about 35 percent Latino and 9 percent African American. Wages in the area for workers are notoriously low, and Texas Tech University, a school with 37,000 students, is located there. Despite all that potential support—a large minority population, a whole lot of students, and workers earning starvation wages—Republicans completely dominate politics in the area, from the local and state to the federal level. In fact, Donald Trump won the county with 66 percent of the vote, while Hillary Clinton received 28 percent. How is that at all possible?

Lubbock County Republicans have stated that the continued GOP domination in the county is a validation of conservative ideals. I doubt that very much. Ask the people of Lubbock whether they want to raise the minimum wage to a living wage. Ask them if they think that health care should be a right, not a privilege, or whether public colleges and universities should be tuition-free. Ask them whether they support comprehensive immigration reform and major changes to our broken criminal justice system. I doubt very much that their answers will be conservative.

The problem is that the Democrats have not shown up and asked those questions. They don't educate. They don't organize. They don't have aggressive voter registration campaigns or get-out-the-vote efforts. And those few Democrats who do try to do the right thing get very little, if any, support from the national Democratic Party. Lubbock, Texas, and hundreds of counties around the country like Lubbock are invisible to national Democrats. For some inexplicable reason, Democrats have thrown in the towel and conceded these areas to right-wing Republicans.

I was in Lubbock to try to begin changing all that, and I hope the wonderful event we did tells the working people there that they are not forgotten.

I told the audience that progressives haven't made their message clear enough in rural America, and that it was the job of everyone there to make their own needs clear, because when 4.5 million Texans have no health insurance, and their state government does not want to expand Medicaid, and their senators voted to end the Affordable Care Act, then the people of Texas should not be voting Republican.

On March 11, we were in Phoenix, Arizona, for another great rally, with two of the most progressive Latino members of Congress, Raúl Grijalva and Ruben Gallego. At that very well-attended event, I had the opportunity of seeing firsthand the racist and anti-immigrant fervor of some of Trump's supporters, who tried to disrupt the meeting. They were not successful, as our security people gently led them outside.

Our trip to Arizona was not all work. In the morning, before the afternoon rally, we had a great time visiting the LA Dodgers spring training camp, located outside Phoenix. The trip was arranged by a staff member who had a connection to the Dodgers organization. I was delighted to be joined by my daughter Heather, who lives in Arizona.

In honor of that visit, my press secretary, Josh Miller-Lewis, handed me a Brooklyn Dodgers hat that had been purchased for the occasion. Of course, why not walk into the LA Dodgers training camp with a Brooklyn Dodgers hat?

Olivia Garvey, a young staff member, was kind enough to show us around the beautiful facility. While the players were in their morning meeting, I walked out to look at the batting cages and practice field. The fans, who had lined up behind the gated fence to see the players, got a bit of a surprise. Instead of Dodger stars like Yasiel Puig and Justin Turner, they got a U.S. senator from Vermont.

Frankly, it's one of those moments you dream of as a kid—walking out onto a baseball field to a cheering crowd. I was delighted to sign baseballs and take selfies and recognize, somewhat belatedly, that I had chosen the wrong profession. My grandchildren were very impressed by a photo of me with Yasiel Puig. In the photo, I am seen instructing him on the fine art of hitting, all based upon my softball days on the playing fields of P.S. 197 in Brooklyn.

I also had the opportunity of talking baseball strategy (not really) with Dodgers manager Dave Roberts. I told him that the Dodgers had played a monumental role in fighting racism when they signed Jackie Robinson to a contract in 1947. Now it was time to end age discrimination in baseball and sign up a seventy-six-year-old shortstop. I didn't convince him.

Proving that one can never get away from politics, while on the field, I chatted a bit with a reporter from the *LA Times* who was covering Dodgers spring training. I mentioned to him that the departure of the Dodgers from Brooklyn, where I was born and raised, was a major political revelation for me. For me as a kid, growing up minutes from Ebbets Field, the Dodgers weren't a team—they were a way of life. Gil Hodges, Pee Wee Reese, Don

Newcombe, Duke Snider, and Jackie Robinson were not only our heroes; they were part of our family.

When the team moved to Los Angeles, I experienced one of my first moments of recognition of the power of corporations and wealthy individuals. Up to then, it had never occurred to me and my friends that an institution like the Brooklyn Dodgers could leave Brooklyn, any more than the Brooklyn Bridge or Prospect Park could leave Brooklyn. It turned out that for the owners of the Dodgers, there was something that mattered more than community: money. It was a lesson I never forgot.

A HELL OF A TWO WEEKS

It has been a hell of a two weeks. I helped write a $1.4 trillion omnibus appropriations bill, held a nationally televised town hall meeting on income and wealth inequality, and brought a resolution to the Senate floor to end the war in Yemen.

Last night, at 1:00 a.m., the Senate passed the appropriations bill. In typical Senate dysfunction, the vote on the bill was delayed for hours because Senator Jim Risch (R-ID) was upset that a wilderness area in his state was being named after a deceased political rival.

Needless to say, this bill, which will affect tens of millions of Americans and is, in many respects, the most important legislation that Congress will pass this year, will get relatively little media coverage. It is not political gossip. It does not deal with the soap opera in the White House or who Trump is hiring or firing. It does not deal with alleged affairs that Trump had with one, two, or three women. It only determines whether people will have enough food to eat, have a roof over their heads, stay warm in the winter, get access to affordable child care, and get the services they need from Social Security, the Department of Veterans Affairs, and myriad other agencies.

From the beginning of the appropriations process, and as a member of the Democratic Leadership, I fought hard to get as much funding as possible for programs that working families desperately needed and that have been underfunded for years. But I wanted a new approach to the appropriations process. In conversations with Democratic Senate leader Chuck Schumer, and in several editorials, I argued that we should highlight a select number of issues that made a clear distinction between the reactionary Republican agenda and what we were trying to accomplish. We had to let the people know that we were fighting to address some of the major problems they were facing. Senator Elizabeth Warren worked with me on this approach. Schumer was in agreement.

Last night the results came in and, given Republican control over the Senate, House, and White House, we did well. Our strategy worked. Much of what I and other progressives fought for was in the bill.

In an op-ed that Senator Warren and I wrote for the *New York Times* on December 17, 2017, three months before the bill was passed, we argued, "Over the past generation, the costs of child care have jumped nearly 1,000 percent. That puts a lot of financial pressure on working parents, and it forces many to make difficult compromises on the quality of care they can afford. If Congress doubles federal support for child care in this year's spending bill, we could guarantee high-quality care for nearly a quarter of a million more children."

Well, last night's bill did just that. It nearly doubled funding for the Child Care and Development Block Grant program.

In our op-ed, we wrote:

Student loan debt is another major burden for many people, including those in lower-paying public service jobs, like teachers, nurses, firefighters, police officers, social workers and military personnel. Ten years ago, Congress created a program to help wipe out student loan debt for these public servants, hoping it would encourage more people to give back to their communities. But because of failures in student loan servicing and a lot of bureaucratic nonsense, many might not get the forgiveness they've earned. Congress can easily fix this in the funding bill and help tens of thousands of people.

The bill provided $350 million in student debt relief for those public servants, part of a $2 billion package to make college more affordable for millions of Americans.

"Social Security is a lifeline in retirement," we said in our op-ed. "But many older people and Americans with disabilities are now struggling to get their benefits because budget cuts have forced the agency running Social Security to cut thousands of jobs and close 64 field offices since 2010. Congress should restore funding to the agency and help fill the gaps in service so that people can get the benefits they have earned."

The bill provided $480 million to the Social Security Administration, the first increase in funding for that agency in almost a decade.

We also were successful in increasing funding for the Department of Veterans Affairs, for treatment for those dealing with opioid addiction, for the Low Income Home Energy Assistance Program, and for many other programs desperately needed by low-income and working families.

Politically, this legislation was a total repudiation of the austerity budget Trump had proposed a few months earlier. He wanted massive cuts in, or the elimination of, virtually every program that was important to the middle class and to low-income families. Instead, we substantially increased funding for these very same programs.

After all my efforts to help shape this legislation, why did I end up voting against it?

This legislation, which I knew had the votes to pass, had two major deficiencies that had to be highlighted. First, it ignored the long-standing crisis facing 1.8 million young people eligible for the DACA program. As I have said many times, this is one of the great moral crises facing our nation, and we cannot rest until it is addressed. With an anti-immigrant Trump as president, an increasing number of these immigrants, who have lived in the United States for virtually their entire lives, face the threat of deportation. We cannot turn our backs on them, and I will continue to do everything I can to provide them with legal protection and a path toward citizenship.

Second, this bill provided a huge $165 billion increase in military spending over the next two years. As a nation already spending well over $600 billion on the military, more than the next ten nations combined, this level of increase was totally unwarranted. We all want a strong defense, but the magnitude of this increase was nothing more than a massive gift to the military-industrial complex. Interestingly, the Department of Defense is the only major agency of government not to have completed an audit, as required by law.

Few contest the fact that waste and fraud within the Defense Department cost us many billions of dollars a year. This is an enormously important issue that most members of Congress are not eager to talk about. I will.

Earlier in the week, on Monday night, my office did something unique. For the first time in history, a U.S. Senate office conducted a town hall meeting in Washington on income and wealth inequality—which was livestreamed to the entire country (and world). The response was extraordinary.

Several months before, we had done our first national town hall meeting on the subject of Medicare for All. It was a great success, with over 1 million people watching live and another million viewing later. This event did even better. Some 1.8 million people saw the program as it was livestreamed, and another 1.2 million people viewed it in the following days. That's a lot of people.

This event, which took place before a standing-room-only audience of 500 at the Capitol Visitor Center, had a great panel, featuring Senator Elizabeth Warren, filmmaker Michael Moore, economist Darrick Hamilton, poverty specialist Catherine Coleman Flowers, UAW vice president Cindy Estrada, and political economist Gordon Lafer. Our ninety-minute discussion focused on the high level of extreme poverty in the country, the collapse of the American middle class over the last forty years, and the incredible power of the Koch brothers and other billionaires to set the agenda for Congress as well as state and local governments. The final segment discussed where we go from here in order to create an economy that works well for all Americans, not just the privileged few.

The purpose of the town hall meetings we hold is to force discussion on issues of huge consequence—issues that, for a variety of reasons, the corporate media largely ignores. My criticism of the corporate media is not that it is "fake news," that it lies all the time or tries to destroy people—which is what Trump believes. My critique is that the corporate media pays relatively little attention to the most important issues facing the working people of our country and increasingly treats politics and government as if they were entertainment or a football game. Over and over again we hear about which politician is "winning" or "losing," or about something stupid that someone said. We hear about the latest polls, Trump's latest tweet, who got fired from the White House this week, and who is arguing with whom in Washington.

Meanwhile, tens of millions of families in this country are struggling to keep their heads above water economically and fail to see a reflection of their reality in the mainstream media. Why are so many people working longer hours for lower wages? Why are we the only major country on earth without guaranteed health care for all? Why are so many Americans living in extreme poverty? What is the impact of climate change on our planet? Why do we pay the highest prices in the world for prescription drugs?

Interestingly, as a sign of the progress we are making on our town hall meetings, our livestream was picked up by the Web pages of CNN, MSNBC, and Fox News—yes, Fox News. Our own Facebook Live reached over 500,000 viewers, and it was also broadcast by such progressive digital partners as the Young Turks, the *Guardian*, NowThis, and Act.TV. While we were not the best-viewed TV program of the evening, we came pretty close. We got 700,000 more viewers than CNN, but lost out to Fox and MSNBC. Given that we're a Senate office and not a TV network, that's not too bad.

The *Huffington Post* got it right in the headline of a piece by Daniel Marans: "The Vermont Senator Is Using His Reach to Try to Shape a National Progressive Narrative." Marans continued: "The broadcast provided the Vermont independent with an opportunity to expand his new alternative media revue beyond 'Medicare for all' to the broader issue of economic inequality, which he maintains that commercial media outlets frequently ignore."

As I said to our friends in the corporate media during the discussion: start paying attention to the reality of how many people in our country are struggling economically every single day—and talk about it.

The next day, Tuesday, March 21, we had another interesting initiative. Along with Republican senator Mike Lee and Democratic senator Chris Murphy, I brought a resolution to the floor of the Senate to end U.S. involvement in the Saudi-led war in Yemen and to change the nature of how Congress does foreign and military policy.

We introduced this resolution for two reasons. First, the war in Yemen has been a humanitarian disaster for the people of that impoverished country. As a result of the war, some 10,000 civilians have been killed, 40,000 more have been wounded, and more than 3 million have been displaced. In November 2017, the United Nations emergency relief coordinator said that Yemen was on the brink of "the largest famine the world has seen for many decades." Fifteen million people lack access to clean water and sanitation because water treatment plants have been destroyed. More than 20 million people in Yemen, over two-thirds of the population, need some kind of humanitarian support, with nearly 10 million in acute need of assistance. More than 1 million suspected cholera cases have been reported, representing potentially the worst cholera outbreak in world history. That is reason enough to end U.S. military support for what Saudi Arabia is doing in the civil war in Yemen.

But the second reason is even more important. We must make

a fundamental change in the way Congress does foreign and military policy. Article 1, Section 8, of the Constitution is very clear. It is Congress that has the responsibility to declare war and send our armed forces into harm's way. Over the years, Congress has, under both Democratic and Republican leadership, abdicated that responsibility and given it over to the president. The time is long overdue for Congress to regain control over this vitally important process, as the founding fathers mandated.

The issue of which body has control over war making and when we send troops into battle is not some abstract intellectual debate. It is of enormous consequence. Anyone who understands the history of American foreign policy knows that, over the years, many of our wars and military interventions were based on lies and deceptions coming from the White House. I'm not just talking about the 1953 CIA/British toppling of Mohammad Mossadegh, the democratically elected prime minister of Iran, and what that has meant to Middle East instability and U.S.-Iran relations. I'm not referring only to the CIA's overthrow of democratically elected Chilean president Salvador Allende, and the fascism that the people there had to endure for years as a result. I am not talking only about the unjust invasions of small countries like Grenada and Panama.

No, I am talking about a process that resulted in the two most significant foreign policy blunders in the modern history of the United States, the war in Iraq and the war in Vietnam. These wars, which were a disaster for hundreds of millions of people throughout the world and deeply affected our own country, occurred when Congress sat back and allowed two administrations, one Republican and one Democrat, to lie to the American people as they led us into unnecessary conflicts with horrific unintended consequences.

We must never allow that to happen again. And that's what our resolution was about.

On March 20, 2003, the war in Iraq, which I had strongly opposed, began, and the bombs started falling on Baghdad. Today, it is widely acknowledged that the Iraq War was a tragedy of enormous magnitude, and that our entry into that war was based on a series of falsehoods. Despite what the Bush administration said, Iraq had no role in the 9/11 attacks, and it did not possess weapons of mass destruction that threatened the United States.

As we now know, that war created a cascade of instability around the region that we are still dealing with today, in Syria and elsewhere, and will be for many years to come. Indeed, had it not been for the Iraq War, the Islamic State would almost certainly not exist. The war deepened hostilities between Sunni and Shiite communities in Iraq and elsewhere. It exacerbated a regional struggle for power between Saudi Arabia and Iran and their proxies in places like Syria, Lebanon, and Yemen, and it undermined American diplomatic efforts to resolve the Israeli-Palestinian conflict.

That war was created by a Republican administration. Now, let me tell you about a Democratic administration, and an earlier conflict that began on similarly false pretenses. In 1964, President Lyndon B. Johnson cited an attack on a U.S. ship in the Gulf of Tonkin as a pretext for escalating the U.S. intervention in Vietnam. We now know from declassified recordings that Johnson himself doubted that the USS *Maddox* had come under fire on August 4, 1964, but he still used that alleged attack to push for the Gulf of Tonkin Resolution, which authorized him to escalate U.S. military involvement in Vietnam. Johnson's administration consistently misled both Congress and the American people into that war, just as the Bush administration misled us into the war in Iraq.

The lesson that must be learned from all of this is that foreign policy disasters occur when presidents refuse to tell their people the truth, and when Congress abdicates its constitutional responsibility to get that truth.

Not surprisingly, the Trump administration, the Republican congressional leadership, and the military establishment strongly opposed our resolution. Secretary of Defense Jim Mattis sent a letter out to members of the Senate explaining his opposition. Senate Majority Leader McConnell held a classified hearing with military and intelligence leaders to gain support to defeat us, and Secretary Mattis himself spoke at both the Republican and Democratic Senate Caucuses on the day of the vote to support the status quo.

Nonetheless, despite all of that opposition, we received 44 votes—from 39 Democrats and 5 Republicans—in support of ending U.S. involvement in the war in Yemen. In voting to table our resolution, the chair and ranking member of the Senate Foreign Relations Committee agreed to hold hearings for the first time on this three-year-old military intervention. I hope that these hearings will happen soon, and that they will ask the necessary tough questions about the administration's justifications for this war. If not, we reserve the right to bring our resolution to the floor of the Senate for consideration again. This is an issue I will not give up on.

I now head home to Vermont for the Easter break and some time with family and friends—which is a good thing. I need to escape the Beltway and recharge.

REMEMBERING DR. KING

I was supposed to get on a plane in Burlington at 5:15 p.m., make a connecting flight in DC at 8:00, and then fly to Memphis for the commemoration of the fiftieth anniversary of the assassination of Dr. Martin Luther King Jr. The bad news was that the plane from Burlington was an hour late. The good news was that the plane from DC was thirty minutes late. I made the connection.

The event was organized by the American Federation of State, County and Municipal Employees (AFSCME), the largest public-sector union in the country. Dr. King was killed in Memphis when he was supporting sanitation workers there who were on strike for better wages, decent working conditions, and the right to be represented by a union.

A month earlier, I met AFSCME president Lee Saunders in my office to talk about the dangerous anti-union *Janus v. AFSCME* case then before the Supreme Court. The goal of that case was to continue the right-wing effort in this country to attack the standard of living of working people, to destroy the trade union movement, and to bring what Republicans call "right to work" to public unions representing municipal and state employees. "Right to work" means the right to work for lower wages and inadequate benefits and allowing workers who benefit from union contracts not to pay union dues. Few doubted that the Republican majority on the Supreme Court would rule against the unions.

During his visit, Saunders mentioned the Memphis event, and I was honored and excited to participate. In my view, Dr. King was one of the outstanding leaders in American history, and his life's work and vision have greatly inspired me and influenced my political thinking. Several years before, I had the honor of speaking at the King Center in Atlanta as part of the King national holiday event. On another occasion, I had the opportunity to discuss Dr. King's life and work with his daughter Bernice. Now I would be in the city where he spent his last hours on earth, with people who believed in what he stood for.

The day's events included a rally that would conclude with a march along the same route that Dr. King and his followers walked fifty years ago with the striking workers. It would take us right past the Mason Temple Church of God in Christ, where King gave his prophetic "I've Been to the Mountaintop" speech—his last.

Along with thousands of others who marched, I walked alongside Dr. King's son; Richard Trumka, president of the American Federation of Labor and Congress of Industrial Organizations (AFL-CIO); James P. Hoffa, president of the International Association of Teamsters; Randi Weingarten, president of the American Federation of Teachers (AFT); Chris Shelton, president of the Communications Workers of America (CWA); Harold A. Schaitberger, president of the International Association of Fire Fighters; and many other labor leaders. The Reverend Al Sharpton and the Reverend William Barber also marched, as did many other civil rights and religious leaders. During the event, I had the honor of meeting some of the now-elderly men who, fifty years earlier, had been on strike in Memphis the day King was assassinated.

In my remarks at the event, I made a point that I have often made. King was a great civil rights leader, largely responsible for ending segregation throughout the South and helping to pass such landmark legislation as the 1964 Civil Rights Act and the 1965 Voting Rights Act. If King and his movement had accomplished nothing more than breaking down the barriers of segregation, he would have been remembered for the ages as one of the great freedom fighters in the history of our country.

But he was more than that. Dr. King was a nonviolent revolutionary who wanted to see our nation undergo "a radical revolution of values," against not just the evils of Jim Crow and segregation but also the triple evils of poverty, racism, and militarism.

Let us never forget that, in an act of incredible courage, King denounced the war in Vietnam. He demanded to know how we could spend billions abroad killing people in an unjust war while ignoring the suffering of millions of people in our own country who were living in dire poverty. He wanted to know how he could advocate nonviolence in America but not oppose the incredible brutality of that war.

His speaking out on the war in Vietnam greatly antagonized the Johnson administration, and alienated much of King's political and financial support from the liberal community. It also engendered mainstream media attacks from those who criticized him for going beyond the only role that they had determined he should play: "civil rights leader." His bold leadership also made mainstream America uncomfortable. A 1966 Gallup poll found that almost two-thirds of Americans had an unfavorable opinion of Dr. King.

Dr. King didn't have to speak out on militarism and the war

and become one of the leaders of the antiwar movement. He didn't have to focus on poverty and income and wealth inequality and organize the Poor People's Campaign. But, with enormous courage, he did.

At a time when the United States spends more on the military, according to a 2018 report by the International Institute for Strategic Studies, than the next ten nations combined, and when we are engaged in never-ending wars, King's opposition to militarism should be something that we learn from. Unfortunately, however, the extent of our huge military budget and our participation in foreign military adventurism remains an issue that few politicians today, Democrats or Republicans, are prepared to discuss.

Dr. King always understood that the "inseparable twin of racial injustice was economic injustice." As he stated in 1968, "What does it profit a man to be able to eat at an integrated lunch counter if he doesn't earn enough money to buy a hamburger and a cup of coffee?" And let us never forget that the great March on Washington that Dr. King led in 1963 was called the March for Jobs and Freedom. For *Jobs* and Freedom.

And we must also remember that the project Dr. King worked on in the last months of his life was the Poor People's Campaign: an effort to bring low-income blacks, whites, Latinos, and Native Americans together to change our national priorities and to create a society where all people could live with dignity and security.

It is my strong view that Dr. King's vision and organizing tactics should continue to guide those of us who want to transform our economic and political systems. Dr. King understood that the only time we bring about real change in this country is when we mobilize people at the grassroots level. Thirty-second TV ads may help win some elections, but they are not going to bring about the fundamental change our country needs.

In Memphis, we also had fun visiting Beale Street, the official home of the blues, where B. B. King performed. There we bumped into my old friend Jesse Jackson, someone I had supported for president back in 1988. We also had great ribs at a local restaurant.

After leaving Memphis, we drove three hours south on I-55 to Jackson, Mississippi, the state capital. I was there to attend a town hall meeting on economic justice we had scheduled with Chokwe Lumumba, the progressive new mayor of the city, which is approximately 81 percent black. The turnout was good, and the discussion was lively.

As a former mayor, I had a lot of empathy for Lumumba and what he was trying to accomplish. While Jackson is an almost all-black city and Burlington is almost all white, many of the issues we faced were similar. Coming from a very poor city in the poorest state in the country, Lumumba had challenges, however, that were more daunting.

The infrastructure in Jackson that the new mayor inherited was a disaster, with huge potholes in the streets and aging water pipes that often broke. With a very limited tax base, Lumumba was struggling with the question of how the city could raise the billions it needed to create a modern urban infrastructure. My belief that, instead of giving huge tax breaks to billionaires, Congress should invest in rebuilding the nation's crumbling infrastructure was something that both Lumumba and the audience strongly agreed with.

In terms of education, Mayor Lumumba struggles with the same challenge that mayors and school boards all across the country face. How do we create twenty-first-century schools that prepare kids for the jobs of the future? How do we develop a pre-K system that adequately prepares children for their future?

As I had learned in the past while visiting African American communities, there is widespread support for the Historically Black Colleges and Universities (HBCU) program. A large percentage of African Americans who have graduate degrees and become leaders in their communities receive their education in these schools.

The mayor informed me that the city is also addressing the vitally important issue of having a broadband system that is fast, reliable, and affordable and that can attract and maintain businesses. We also discussed how Jackson could make sure that low-income people got the health care they need, especially in a state that did not expand Medicaid.

What I especially liked about Mayor Lumumba was his emphasis on participatory democracy and involving ordinary people in the process of running government. He had created "people's assemblies" and councils to help address the major issues facing the community and was reaching out aggressively to young people.

Politically, based on its racial history, it goes without saying that Mississippi is a very unusual state. In 2012, Barack Obama received almost 44 percent of the vote in Mississippi for his reelection. This happened despite the fact that the national Democratic Party put little money and energy into the state. While Obama won the overwhelming percentage of the black vote, he won only 10 percent of the white vote. This is absurd. There is little doubt in my mind that if Democrats develop a fifty-state strategy, and stop ignoring states like Mississippi, we can both increase black voter turnout and win a much higher percentage of white votes.

Let me go out on a limb here. I believe that within the decade, Mississippi not only may go from red to blue but could become one of the most progressive states in the country. It will take work. It will take money. But it can be done.

April 13, 2018

THE POLITICAL REVOLUTION
IS LOOKING GREAT

I had hoped to get out of Washington in the afternoon and back to Burlington for a busy weekend. Out of nowhere, however, votes were scheduled in the late afternoon and I couldn't get a plane out earlier than 10:10 p.m.—not my favorite flight.

Although it had been a long day, I was a happy camper as I boarded the plane. A few hours earlier, I had spoken at a wonderful and inspiring event: a four-day training session for 450 candidates from 48 states, teaching them how they could run effective campaigns and win elections. These candidates were running for school board, city council, county commission, state legislature, governor, and Congress—64 percent of them in districts Trump won in 2016. They were white, black, Latino, Asian American, and Native American. They were straight and gay. They were women and men (slightly more women), young and older. They were running in red states, purple states, and blue states, nearly every state in the country. They were campaigning in communities that Trump won, and places that were overwhelmingly Democratic. And what was most exciting was that 82 percent of them had never run for political office before.

Most important, they were all campaigning on progressive agendas. During my run for president, I had talked about the need for a political revolution, about building a movement and getting new people involved in the political process and running for office. Well, this was it, the political revolution in action. And this type of activity was taking place not only in training sessions in Washington, but also all across the country, as more and more candidates were running for office and more and more people were becoming involved in politics.

My view is, and has always been, that campaigns are not just about the candidate. They are about understanding that real change never comes from the top down, but always from the grassroots on up. So, it was enormously gratifying to see that process unfolding right before my eyes. This is how we are going to transform America.

This training covered the rudiments of how to be a successful candidate at any level, including: How do you put together a strong campaign staff and bring in volunteers? How do you raise money? How do you do press releases and social media? How do you get local endorsements? How do you determine what issues are important to your community? How do you do well in debates and public speaking? In other words, information was being supplied to people whose families and backgrounds were not part of the political establishment and, under normal circumstances, would not have given a second thought to running for office.

During my remarks, I urged the candidates to focus on a few basic things. First, talk about the issues that are relevant to the people you hope to represent. More often than not, those concerns related to decent-paying jobs, health care, education, and the environment. I also suggested, if they were running for local office, that the most important thing that they and their campaign co-workers could do was to knock on as many doors as possible, because there is nothing more effective than face-to-face contact. TV, radio, and digital ads are important, but having a discussion with a constituent in his or her kitchen is far more impactful. I also urged the candidates not to become overly reliant on consultants and pollsters—people who often make large amounts of money from campaigns and who usually bring forth tired, old boilerplate concepts. I told them to trust their own instincts, be themselves, and bring as many people as possible into the campaign.

Training sessions like the one I attended do not happen by accident. It takes an enormous amount of work to organize them, successfully put them on, and then do the appropriate follow-up work. This event was sponsored by two grassroots organizations, the Progressive Change Campaign Committee and Our Revolution.

Brianna Westbrook, an automotive sales representative now running for a seat in Arizona's state senate, told ABC News, "The political climate has been turned upside down, and I give credit to Bernie Sanders for that. You have working-class people standing up and running for office, and that is more important than ever."

I'm happy to give the credit back to her for running. As I have said many times, elections are not going to be won unless there is excitement on the ground, unless ordinary people become involved. In 2014, when Republicans won landslide victories, the national voter turnout was the lowest since World War II, with only 37 percent of the people voting. People were disillusioned, mistrustful, and alienated from the political process.

What I saw at this campaign training session in Washington, and what is taking place all across the country, tells me that this situation is changing. People are angry that we have a president like Donald Trump, angry that we have a U.S. Congress more concerned about the needs of billionaires than of ordinary Americans, and they are fighting back.

It is a beautiful sight to behold.

JUMPING INTO CONTROVERSY

On domestic policy—taxation, health care, the environment, education, criminal justice, immigration, and so forth—there are major differences between the Democratic Party and the Republican Party. On foreign policy, not so much. In fact, a number of observers have correctly pointed out that, to a very great degree, we have a "one-party foreign policy." As a result, there is almost no debate about the basic premises underlying our long-term foreign policy positions. In a complicated and volatile world, this is not a good thing.

Several months ago, Democrats, with virtually no opposition, gave President Trump every nickel that he wanted in increased defense spending. At a time when our infrastructure is crumbling, when public schools lack the resources to provide a quality education for our kids, when 30 million people have no health insurance, there were very few Democrats opposed to Republican efforts to increase military spending by $165 billion over two years.

Democrats, for good reason, vehemently oppose almost everything Trump proposes, but when he asks for a huge increase in military spending, there are almost no voices in dissent. Why is that? Do we really have to spend more on the military than the next ten nations combined—most of which are our allies? Why do we dramatically increase funding for the military when the Department of Defense remains the only major government agency not to have undertaken a comprehensive audit? Why is there so little discussion about the billions in waste, fraud, and cost overruns at the Pentagon?

Sixty years ago, President Dwight D. Eisenhower warned us about the dangerous influence of the military-industrial complex. The situation since then has only gotten worse. Is anyone paying attention?

But it's not just military spending. If most Democrats now conclude that the "war on drugs" has been a criminal justice disaster for our country, why is there not a similar examination of the "war on terror"? Year after year, we continue the same old strategy of fighting terrorism. But very few people are analyzing the results of those ongoing policies.

Seventeen years after we entered Afghanistan, about 15 million people—half the population—are living in areas that either are controlled by the Taliban or where the Taliban are openly present and regularly mount attacks. That doesn't sound to me like a great success story.

Fifteen years after we "shocked and awed" our way into Iraq and overthrew Saddam Hussein, the Iraqi government is now largely under the political influence of Iran. Ironically, U.S. policy helped create for Iran what they were unable to accomplish for themselves in their long and bloody war with Iraq. While the United States now spends billions in military aid opposing Iran, Iranian-sponsored militias are now active in Iraq, helping to move men and guns to proxy forces in Syria and Lebanon.

The "war on terror" in Iraq, Afghanistan, Syria, and Yemen has cost the United States thousands of lives and trillions of dollars. These wars have caused massive destabilization in the region, the deaths of many hundreds of thousands of people there, and the displacement of millions who were driven from their homelands. Further, these wars have significantly impacted Europe, which has seen the rise of right-wing extremist movements in response to the mass migration of refugees into those countries.

For decades now, in the extremely volatile Gulf region, the United States has determined that our major "ally" in the region is Saudi Arabia, a despotic autocracy controlled by an extremely wealthy family that treats women as third-class citizens, jails dissidents, ruthlessly exploits the foreign labor that keeps its economy going, and has exported the extremist Islamic doctrine of Wahhabism around the world. Why have we continued to give them unconditional support while they and their Gulf allies work diligently to suppress democracy across the region? Why have we continued to sell them billions of dollars' worth of sophisticated weapons while they wage a ruthless war in Yemen?

How does it happen that there is almost no debate as to why we have determined that Saudi Arabia is the "good guy" in that area while Iran is the "bad guy"? This was the position of the 2016 Democratic candidate for president, Hillary Clinton. This is the position of the Republican president, Donald Trump. Is it the right position?

Foreign policy is not easy stuff, especially at a time when multibillionaire, authoritarian kleptocrats have growing political and economic power in America and around the world. It's an area that needs more public and congressional discussion. It's a subject where basic long-term assumptions need to be challenged. Doing the same old same old does not make sense.

On April 16, I spoke to several thousand people who attended the J Street annual conference, including many young Jewish students.

J Street is a liberal Jewish organization. It was founded in 2007 to provide an alternative voice to the American Israel Public Affairs Committee (AIPAC), the powerful conservative Jewish organization whose views on Israel have enormous influence over Congress. Its goal is to promote American leadership to end the Arab-Israeli and Israeli-Palestinian conflicts peacefully and diplomatically.

In my remarks, I stated a view that very few in Congress, Republican or Democrat, are prepared to express, for fear of being called "anti-Israel." My speech was an effort not only to shine a new light on how we should address the never-ending conflicts in the Middle East, but also to open up a debate on this issue beyond the one-party approach that is now dominant.

> My friends, the issues that we are dealing with are enormously complicated. Nobody I know has any simple or magical answers to them, and real solutions will require a great deal of hard work. But what I do know is that the United States of America should lead the world with a foreign policy which emphasizes the need to bring nations together, which focuses on diplomacy and international cooperation, rather than a foreign policy that emphasizes the continued use of military force.
>
> And let me also say this. As someone who believes absolutely and unequivocally in Israel's right to exist, and to exist in peace and security, as someone who as a young man lived in Israel for a number of months and is very proud of his Jewish heritage, as someone who is deeply concerned about the global rise of anti-Semitism and all forms of racism,

we must say loudly and clearly that to oppose the reactionary policies of Prime Minister Netanyahu does not make us anti-Israel.

I also referenced the ongoing conflict in Gaza, a crisis that had just erupted into violence as large Palestinian protests were met with an armed response by the Israeli military, with over 30 Palestinians killed. I discussed the horrific economic problems facing Gaza, where 2 million people live in a densely crowded area with highly polluted drinking water, where youth unemployment is at 60 percent, and where freedom of movement is highly curtailed.

I told the audience that I had condemned Hamas's use of terrorist violence and would continue to do so. But that violence cannot excuse shooting at unarmed protesters, and it cannot excuse trapping nearly 2 million people inside Gaza. In my view, the United States must play a much more aggressive and even-handed role in ending the Gaza blockade and helping Palestinians and Israelis build a future that works for all. And if the White House is unable to do that, Congress must take the lead.

I also felt it necessary to raise another point, one that is very rarely discussed. While we rightfully criticize the Netanyahu government for its obstructionism and for its unwillingness to seriously negotiate with the Palestinians, we must also demand that incredibly wealthy regional states and kingdoms in the area play a new and much more positive role in helping to rebuild Gaza and bring stability to the region.

I concluded:

I read a story the other day about the crown prince of Saudi Arabia. He was just in the United States for a visit, and you might have seen one of the fifty different TV and magazine interviews he did. In any case, as I understand it, the crown prince recently purchased a $500 million yacht because he thought it looked nice. And I'm sure it did. This is on top of his owning the world's most expensive mansion—worth some $300 million.

So I say to the crown prince and the other multibillionaire leaders in the region, stop just talking about the poverty and distress in Gaza—do something meaningful about it. I heard the other day that the Saudi king pledged $50 million to UNRWA, the UN agency that works with Palestinian refugees. Fifty million dollars is not a small sum of money, but let us not forget that it is 10 percent of what the crown prince paid for a yacht.

THE FIGHT FOR A MORAL ECONOMY

The Rev. William Barber II is a man who impresses me deeply. He is an African American civil rights leader, based in North Carolina, who has done an extraordinary job in bringing people together from all backgrounds and all races in the fight for justice. His "Moral Monday" rallies outside the North Carolina state house have attracted as many as 80,000 people as he has helped lead the opposition to the draconian policies of that state's right-wing government. From a political perspective, he is widely credited for having played a major role in helping a Democrat win an upset victory in the governor's race in the 2016 election. I believe that my friend Dr. Cornel West is right when he states that "William Barber is the closest person we have to Martin Luther King Jr. in our midst."

I had invited Reverend Barber to do a podcast with me in Washington, and we made plans to do a meeting together in North Carolina. When the event, to be held at Duke University in Durham on January 19, was announced, it sold out in minutes. Unfortunately, the event had to be postponed at the last minute because I had to remain in Washington to deal with the threat of another government shutdown by the Republicans. The event was rescheduled for April 19, 2018, and entitled, "The Enduring Challenge of a Moral Economy: 50 Years After Dr. King Challenged Racism, Poverty, and Militarism."

Being up on a stage with Reverend Barber is an inspiring experience, but it is also challenging. It's not easy to keep up with someone who is brilliant, passionate, and able to quote the Bible at will to amplify his point. This is also a man who, his audience understands, does more than just lecture or preach. He has been at the forefront in struggle after struggle and has been arrested dozens of times in nonviolent actions.

In fact, just before we entered the Duke chapel for the event, I had the opportunity to witness firsthand some of the humanitarian work Reverend Barber does that crosses racial and cultural boundaries. We accompanied him to a local church that was providing sanctuary for José Chicas, an undocumented pastor who has been living in this country for thirty-three years, has a wife and four children, and presides over a Latino church in Raleigh. For decades, Pastor Chicas had signed in with the proper federal authorities, paid his taxes, and had a work permit. Under the Trump administration, however, the pastor was slated for deportation, to be separated forever from his family and his congregation.

Reverend Barber and the clergyman who was helping Pastor Chicas and his family asked us to try to publicize the pastor's situation. We taped a discussion we had at the sanctuary location with Pastor Chicas and his family. It received well over 800,000 views on our Facebook page.

It is Reverend Barber's deep conviction that there should not be a separation between one's religious beliefs and sense of morality and one's approach to politics. In fact, he stated in his podcast with me that "I was taught that there is no separation between justice and Jesus. Any attempt to separate the two is heresy." During our conversation at Duke, his harshest words were aimed at those religious figures who preach the Bible every Sunday, but somehow turn a blind eye to the pain, suffering, and injustice that take place in their communities and in their country.

During our discussion and the question-and-answer period, he also made clear the absolute necessity to bring together people of all races and backgrounds in the fight for economic, social, and racial justice. He expressed very strongly how demagogues in our country were winning elections by dividing poor and working-class whites, who are in desperate need of decent-paying jobs, health care, and educational opportunities for their kids—from people of color and immigrants.

During our discussion at Duke, Reverend Barber made it clear that he is following in Dr. King's footsteps in attempting the very difficult effort to organize a national Poor People's Campaign. A view that he and I shared was that politicians and the media cannot continue to ignore the reality of poverty in America, not when tens of millions of families—black, white, Latino, Asian American, and Native American—are struggling every day to survive economically.

As I left him, Reverend Barber handed me a copy of *The Poverty and Justice Bible*. It's compelling reading.

On Friday morning, my staff and I boarded a plane from Durham to New York City, where I was scheduled to speak before the National Action Network, a major civil rights organization founded and led by the Reverend Al Sharpton. Later in the day, I was to meet with some political reporters at the *New York Times*, do a TV segment with Chris Hayes of MSNBC, and congratulate JetBlue workers at LaGuardia Airport who had just voted to form a union. Then, on a late flight out, I was on my way back to Burlington.

The speech I gave at the National Action Network attempted to address both the crisis of institutional racism and the national policies that were needed to improve the economic conditions of the African American community—and all Americans. The conference focused on taking "a look back on the last 50 years since Reverend Dr. Martin Luther King's assassination in 1968." In other words, we had to get beyond the alleged conflict between fighting racial injustice versus fighting economic injustice. We must deal with both. In that regard, I quoted Dr. King, who understood that the "inseparable twin of racial injustice is economic injustice."

As I told the audience, for me, remembering Dr. King is remembering the need to end institutional racism, end poverty, end militarism, radically change our national priorities, and create a government that works for all of us.

In discussing Trump, I made it clear that my major concern about him was not just his horrendous and reactionary views on taxation, health care, climate change, education, women's rights, etc., and his overall policies, which are designed to represent the billionaire class at the expense of almost everyone else. It goes deeper than that.

I told the audience:

My major criticism is that he is doing what no president in modern history has done. He is trying, aggressively and for cheap political gain, to divide us up based on the color of our skin, the country we were born in, our gender, our sexual orientation, or our religion. Maybe we should not be surprised that someone who helped lead the birther movement and claimed that Barack Obama was born in Kenya, or someone who referred to Haiti and African countries as "shitholes," is attempting to do this, but it is outrageous and un-American nonetheless.

I also made it clear that no one can speak of a "strong economy" without understanding what institutional racism has meant for the economic life of the African American community. I stated:

> We can't talk about an economy doing well when 21 percent of African Americans are living in poverty, a poverty rate that is two and a half times the rate for the white community. We can't talk about a strong economy when 34 percent of black children live in poverty, almost three times the rate for white kids, or when the infant mortality rate for black infants is more than double the rate for white infants. We can't talk about a healthy society when black high school graduates have a real unemployment rate of 42 percent.
>
> We can't talk about justice in this country when the median white family has $171,000 in wealth, while the median black family has just $17,000 in wealth—a wealth gap of ten to one. We can't talk about real economic progress when 53 percent of black workers make less than $15 an hour. And we can't talk about being a nation of opportunity when social mobility is so much easier for young whites than young African Americans.

It was also imperative for me to speak about criminal justice, something that groups like Black Lives Matter had brought to the fore. In my remarks I said:

When we talk about the major problems facing our country we must talk about a broken criminal justice system deeply infused with racism. This is the United States of America. We should not have more people in prison than any country on earth, including China.

We should not be spending $80 billion a year to lock up 2.2 million Americans, disproportionately African American, Latino, and Native American, who are imprisoned at more than five times the rate of whites.

We should not tolerate a situation in which, if current trends continue, one in four black males born today can expect to spend time in prison during their lifetime or where young black males are nine times more likely to be killed by police officers than other Americans, while rates of police killings for Native American and Latino men are also disproportionately high. We must not accept a reality where, according to the Department of Justice, blacks were three times more likely to be searched during a traffic stop compared to white motorists.

I also talked about how we needed to end the war on drugs, which has been a forty-year failure, especially for minority communities, and about the progress being made around the country to decriminalize and/or legalize marijuana.

CRIMINAL JUSTICE, POLITICS, AND PENNSYLVANIA

Pennsylvania voted for Trump. It's a state, therefore, that I wanted to spend some time in. It's also a state in which some very important work is being done in criminal justice reform that I needed to learn about. So I traveled there on May 4 to participate in a forum on criminal justice, then to speak in support of three progressive candidates who were on the ballot in the Pennsylvania Democratic primaries on May 15.

At the forum, which was broadcast on cable in Philadelphia, I was joined by Larry Krasner, the city's newly elected district attorney, who had been supported by Our Revolution in his campaign; Premal Dharia, the director of litigation for Civil Rights Corps; and Keeanga-Yamahtta Taylor, an assistant professor of African American Studies at Princeton University.

The discussion was interesting and the subject matter enormously important. The bad news is our criminal justice system not only is deeply broken but often punishes people for simply being black, brown, poor, uneducated, or mentally ill. The good news is we're beginning to talk about the need for criminal justice reform, and we're making some progress.

Today in America, more than 2 million people are in jail, disproportionately black, Latino, and Native American. That is a greater number of inmates than in any other country on earth—including China, which has a population four times greater than ours and an authoritarian government that does not tolerate dissent. Unbelievably, at the local, state, and federal levels, we now spend some $80 billion a year locking up our fellow Americans.

This is what a broken criminal justice system looks like, and it is what we discussed at the forum.

In the middle of 2016, there were 740,700 inmates in city and county jails. Over 65 percent of these inmates were "unconvicted." If they had not been convicted of a crime, why were they in jail? Good question. Answer: Because a majority of them could not afford bail and were forced to remain imprisoned as they awaited trial. Nationally, nearly half of felony defendants cannot make bail, and they stay in jail until their case is heard. The average length of a stay in jail for them is twenty-five days, but people can be held significantly longer awaiting trial.

Do you remember the conclusion to the Pledge of Allegiance? "With liberty and justice for all." Nice words. Unfortunately, that's not how it works now. Today, we have a two-tier criminal justice system. If you are wealthy or middle class, you post bail and prepare for your trial at home. If you are poor and cannot afford the $500 or $1,000 for bail, you are forced to remain in jail while you await your trial.

But that's not all. In case you didn't know it, we still have the equivalent of debtors' prisons in the United States. There are tens of thousands of Americans now in jail because they are too poor to pay a traffic ticket or some other municipal fine. When people can't pay those fines, cities arrest and keep them, sometimes for weeks, in jail.

How crazy is that? Why would anyone want to make a bad situation even worse for struggling Americans? If these low-income people happen to be working, jail time will likely result in the loss of their jobs and the inadequate income they currently have. If they are struggling to pay rent, jail time could mean the loss of their house or apartment and lead to homelessness. In the year 2018, people should not be imprisoned because they can't pay a municipal fine.

But that's not all. It is clear that after almost fifty years of the war on drugs, we can conclude that this war has been a dismal failure and, as in many other wars, countless lives have been destroyed. If you can believe it, in 2018, the Controlled Substances Act continues to treat both marijuana and heroin equally as Schedule 1 substances. You may like marijuana or you may not, but very few informed people believe that marijuana should be treated similarly to a killer drug like heroin.

And yet, in 2016, there were approximately 587,000 arrests for marijuana—roughly one per minute. The American Civil Liberties Union (ACLU) reports that from 2001 to 2010, there were 8.2 million marijuana arrests, 88 percent of them for simple possession. Further, the war on drugs has significant racial implications.

Despite similar usage rates, blacks are almost four times as likely as whites to be arrested for marijuana.

The reality is that if you have a police record, for possession of marijuana or anything else, it will be harder to get a job, find an apartment, or get admitted to a school. How many young people's lives got off to a bad start because of a police record related to marijuana?

The good news is that many states and cities across the country are taking action to undo the damage caused by the war on drugs. More and more states are moving to decriminalize or legalize the possession of marijuana, and some have passed legislation to expunge prior misdemeanor convictions. The prohibition of alcohol in the 1920s was a failed policy. The prohibition of marijuana has also failed.

It will shock no one, I suspect, to learn that the vast majority of people in jail are not only poor but have limited levels of education. The Literacy Project Foundation has found, for example, that fully 85 percent of juvenile offenders have trouble reading. It costs significantly more money to incarcerate someone than to send that person to college. Wouldn't it make sense for us to invest in education and job training rather than in jails and incarceration?

We have also turned our prisons into de facto mental health facilities. According to the Bureau of Justice Statistics, more than one-third of all prison inmates have prior diagnoses of a mental health disorder, including 66 percent of all female prisoners. Many of the inmates were diagnosed with depression or bipolar disorder.

Mental illness and addiction are not crimes. They are illnesses, and they should be treated as such. We could save many lives and billions of dollars if we recognized that simple reality.

I was impressed by the views that District Attorney Krasner expressed at the forum, and even more impressed by what he is actually doing on the job. Shaun King, a writer for the Intercept, reviewed Krasner's new and innovative approaches to criminal justice. As part of his effort to reduce the prison population in Philadelphia, King wrote,

> *Krasner instructed his prosecutors to now add up and justify the exact costs of every single person sentenced to a crime in Philadelphia. Stating that the city is currently spending an*

astounding $360 million per year to jail around just 6,000
people, Krasner then gave examples of all of the things that such
money could be doing in the city currently. Stating that it costs
between $42,000 and $60,000 per year to incarcerate a person,
he reminded the prosecutors that the average total family income
of a person in the city was just $41,000. The annual cost of
incarceration, Krasner reminded his prosecutors, was currently
more per year than the beginning salary of teachers, police
officers, firefighters, social workers, addiction counselors, and
even prosecutors in his office.

When we talk about criminal justice reform, that discussion must include police department reform. All of us want to live in safe communities, want to keep dangerous people off the streets, and want to see criminals apprehended. That means we need to have good police departments with well-trained, well-paid professionals on the job who are proud of the important work they do.

As a former mayor who worked closely with the Burlington Police Department, I am more than aware that a police officer's job is extremely difficult and dangerous, and that officers are forced to make life-or-death decisions in a split second. For that reason, in supporting our police, it's important that we get the bad apples out of police work and provide increased training for those who want to do the best job possible for their communities.

Lethal force should be the last response, not the first response. Almost all Americans have been shocked and dismayed by video after video on TV showing police officers shooting unarmed people, often black or Latino.

Police officers spend far, far more hours learning how to use their weapon than learning de-escalation tactics or how to deal with mentally ill people acting out. That has got to change.

Lastly, when we talk about criminal justice reform and the outrageously high rate of incarceration in our country, let us not forget about the profound political impact that has on our democracy. Today, 6 million Americans have lost their right to vote because of felony disenfranchisement. Nearly one-quarter of them live in Florida, including one in five otherwise eligible African American voters in the state. In Florida, Kentucky, Tennessee, and Virginia, more than one in five African Americans are disenfranchised. Overall, one in thirteen African American adults is disenfranchised (7.4 percent).

The personal, social, and economic costs of our current justice system are too high to bear any longer.

The next day, I spoke at two rallies for congressional candidates. On a sunny morning in a park in Lancaster, I joined Jess King, a candidate from the Eleventh District, speaking to almost 3,000 people. It was a beautiful event, with people from all ages and backgrounds. There was a lot of energy there. Later in the day, I traveled to Allentown for another well-attended event with a great candidate for Congress, Greg Edwards. But I want to focus on our rally for John Fetterman on Friday, after the forum.

Fetterman is the mayor of Braddock, Pennsylvania, a working-class city in the western part of the state. He is six-eight, has a shaved head, has tattoos on his arms, and rarely wears a tie—and is a strong progressive who supported my presidential campaign. I first met John when he and I campaigned together in Pennsylvania in 2016 for the Democratic candidate for U.S. Senate. I liked him. He recently asked me to help him out in his bid to become lieutenant governor. I was glad to do it. Given that he was from Western Pennsylvania, and better known there, we decided to do the rally in Philadelphia, where he needed to raise his profile.

As 6:00 p.m. approached, the time for the rally to begin, we had about 2,500 people out in front of City Hall—a good crowd. The format was simple. John's wife introduced him. He introduced me, and I was to speak.

Before I got up to the podium, however, a supporter informed me that there was somebody in the crowd with a bullhorn who intended to disrupt my speech. With that warning in the back of my mind, I went up to the platform and began speaking. Sure enough, a few minutes into my remarks, there was the sound of a voice through a loud bullhorn. It was coming from behind me, and the intention was to try to drown me out.

Dealing with hecklers or people trying to disrupt my speeches is not something that I am unfamiliar with. Heckling happens fairly often. Just a few months before Philadelphia, the police had dragged about a dozen right-wing anti-immigration protesters out of a rally we did in Phoenix.

In my experience, the best way to deal with those trying to disrupt our events is to ignore them and speak right over them. I have the microphone. They don't. Plus, I'm pretty loud in any case. So I kept talking, trying not to get distracted from my message, not looking back in the direction of the heckler.

Eventually, however, I sensed that a commotion of sorts was taking place right behind me—actually, on the stage. Voices were raised, and I could feel the vibration of heavy steps and scuffling. It was all very unusual, but I kept on talking. Fifteen minutes later, my remarks completed, I left the platform and headed back to the car. I noticed that there were more police in the area than when I had entered.

What I had missed was a man with a megaphone leaping up onto the platform. While I was oblivious to it all, the local CBS affiliate described the action.

PHILADELPHIA (CBS)—A protester was taken away in handcuffs during a Bernie Sanders rally in Philadelphia on Friday night. Senator Sanders was in town rallying for John Fetterman, who is a Democratic candidate running for Lieutenant Governor in Pennsylvania.

Moments after Sanders began speaking to the crowd, a man wearing a white t-shirt and a black bandana can be seen jumping up onto the platform attempting to use a megaphone. After several unsuccessful attempts at disrupting the rally, the protester was taken off the stage in handcuffs. Police could not confirm if any charges were being filed.

The TV report neglected to mention that the protester had chained himself to a fence on the stage, and that the police had had to use heavy-duty chain cutters to get him off before taking him away in handcuffs.

Here is what drives me nuts about media coverage. Over 2,500 people attend a rally. A U.S. senator gives a speech. No coverage of what he says. A candidate for lieutenant governor gives a speech. No coverage of what he says. One protester takes out a bullhorn, gets arrested, and that's the coverage. That's bad. What's even crazier is that nobody even knew what this guy was protesting!

A BUSY WEEKEND IN VERMONT

Sometimes when I'm in the DC airport heading back to Vermont, the people I talk to assume that I'm heading home for a weekend of fun and relaxation. The truth is that I often work harder on weekends in Vermont than I do during the week in Washington. The difference is that being back in Vermont, no matter what I'm doing, is almost always more fun.

This weekend we had three major events in Vermont. On Friday, my office put together our sixth town hall meeting of the year with Vermont high school students. The meeting was held at the Essex Career Center, in Essex Junction, Vermont.

There are several serious problems that we're trying to address with these meetings. Vermont does better than average in terms of the percentage of our kids who graduate high school. We do worse than average, however, in the percentage of our kids who go on to college. We are also weak in the kind of apprenticeship and career training programs we offer high school graduates who are not planning on pursuing higher education. Working with the state government and Vermont nonprofit organizations, I was determined to find out why that was the case and what we could do about it.

It is my long-held view that we must extend the concept of public education beyond the twelfth grade and make public colleges and universities tuition-free. Every young person, regardless of the income of his or her family, should have the opportunity to get the education they need to get a decent job and make it into the middle class. This is good not only for the young people themselves, but for the economy as well. Several decades ago, the United States was regarded as the best-educated country on earth, as we led the world in the percentage of our people who had college degrees. Today, we are in tenth place. In a highly competitive global economy, that is not the place we want to be in.

While I continue to fight to make public colleges and universities tuition-free, and we're seeing some positive movement in this regard around the country, we're not there yet. So, one of my tasks, as Vermont's senator, is to do everything I can to help young people and their parents know what kind of financial aid is available now and how they can make the best choices possible as to what college might work for them. Many kids, especially those whose parents never went to college, are intimidated by the college admission and financial aid process, and some give up in frustration. I wanted to use these meetings to break down those fears and get out as much information as possible.

One part of the problem we are confronting in Vermont, especially in the smaller schools, is that many of the high school guidance counselors simply do not have sufficient time to help college-bound students deal with issues of college choice or financial aid because they are spending more time than ever with student behavioral problems. Not surprisingly, kids who are disrupting classrooms or who have serious family problems get seen first. While this is understandable, it is not fair to the young people and their families who are struggling with complicated and intimidating forms. We need to strengthen the guidance counselor system in Vermont and, I suspect, throughout the country.

At our student town hall meetings, we brought knowledgeable people in to talk about the different types of grants available from the federal government, nonprofit organizations, and the military; what kinds of scholarships were available from different colleges around the state; and how families go about applying for student loans. We also made it possible for parents and kids to speak directly after the meetings with experts who could help them fill out the necessary forms.

We heard some inspiring stories. At a meeting in northern Vermont, a recent high school graduate from a low-income family explained how she was able to attend one of the best and most expensive colleges in the country, Middlebury College, without any cost to her or her family because of the school's generous scholarship program. In fact, many colleges have strong financial aid packages, and it was important for kids to understand that those programs existed.

At another meeting, a local doctor talked about how, despite coming from a working-class family, she had been able to put together financial aid packages that enabled her to make it through medical school and pursue the career she always wanted.

Another, very brave high school student talked about her fears, her lack of self-confidence, and the psychological assaults she endured from her parents, who kept telling her that she was not smart enough to go to college. For many low-income kids, the struggle to obtain a college education is not just financial. It also has to do with self-esteem issues. Many do not believe that they have the intelligence or the ability to succeed in college. As the son of working-class parents who never went to college, I was not unfamiliar with those feelings.

Importantly, not every high school kid wants to go to college or has the academic skills necessary to do well in higher education. Some of these young people are great with their hands but not so good with books. Too often, these students are disrespected, stereotyped, and regarded as second-class citizens. That's wrong. It's not only unfair to these young people but very much against the best economic interests of our country.

Earlier in the year, I brought the ambassador from Germany to Vermont. He was able to explain to the governor, members of the legislature, teachers, and the general public how the internationally regarded German apprenticeship program works. At a time when Vermont and the country desperately need such skilled workers as carpenters, welders, plumbers, electricians, mechanics, and machinists, we have a lot to learn from the Germans. At two of our town hall meetings, I brought a number of employers directly into the high schools to explain to the students what kind of good-paying jobs were available and how they could get the necessary training for them.

On a Saturday morning at Norwich University, in Northfield, Vermont, we dealt with a very different subject. We held a statewide town hall meeting for Vermont veterans. As a longtime member of the U.S. Senate Committee on Veterans' Affairs, and as the former chair of that committee, I have worked for years with the veterans community in Vermont and around the country on issues of concern to them. I am proud to be the recipient of the highest national awards offered by the American Legion and the Veterans of Foreign Wars (VFW) for my work on veterans' issues.

In Vermont, over the years, we have made significant improvements in VA health care, including the creation of a women's clinic at the VA Medical Center at White River Junction. We have also expanded the number of primary-care veterans' clinics around the state from three to five, and upgraded most of them.

The purpose of this town hall meeting was to inform Vermont veterans about the benefits they were entitled to, discuss with them what was going on in Washington, and hear their concerns. As part of the opening panel, we had representatives from the major service organizations in the state—the American Legion, the VFW, the Vietnam Veterans of America, and the Disabled American Veterans. The director of the VA Medical Center in Vermont was also on the panel. Our keynote speaker was the national legislative director of the American Legion, the largest veterans organization in the country.

The VA health care system, with 137 medical centers, located in almost every state, is the largest integrated health care provider in the country. In recent years, the VA has received an enormous amount of public criticism, some deserved and some not deserved. As a huge $200 billion-a-year federal bureaucracy, the VA moves far too slowly in addressing the needs of veterans. In addition, there is no question but that some of the medical centers around the country have provided inadequate care and forced veterans to wait far too long for the care they needed. That's simply true and is an issue that cannot be ignored.

On the other hand, what is also true is that study after study has found that the quality of care at the VA is as good as, or better than, that provided in the private sector. The VA has been a health care pioneer in many areas, including patient safety, the use of telemedicine, and the provision of holistic care. Further, the VA health care system is enormously popular with veterans, who appreciate that the mission of the VA is to take care of their medical needs, not to make a profit off them. Veterans also like the idea that many of the staff are veterans themselves or people related to veterans who understand their often unique problems. Time after time, I have heard from veterans, for example, about how hard it is to talk about post-traumatic stress disorder (PTSD) with medical personnel who have little understanding of what it is like to be on a battlefield.

We should also understand that a lot of the criticism directed at the VA health care system has nothing to do with the quality of care provided but everything to do with politics. Let's be clear. The VA is a socialized health care system, owned and operated by the U.S. government. It provides free or inexpensive care to millions of Americans and enables them to purchase prescription drugs for a very low price. In case you haven't noticed, there are a lot of Republicans who are not wildly sympathetic to socialized medicine. (In fact, these are the same people who tried to throw 32 million Americans off Obamacare and want massive cuts to Medicare, Medicaid, and other public health programs.)

In my view, the long-term goal of Republicans is to significantly privatize the VA health care system. They want to cut back on VA-provided services and push veterans into private care, which they'll do, I suspect, by converting the VA into a voucher system, with veterans picking up a larger and larger percentage of the cost. In fact, Dr. David Shulkin was recently fired by President Trump as secretary of the VA because he was not moving the privatization process fast enough.

Most veterans, however, don't want this. In my discussions with them at the town hall meeting, and during the question-and-answer period that followed, they expressed strong support for the care they were getting and, like all of the major veterans organizations, opposed privatization.

In terms of veterans' issues, the good news is that the American people have learned a very important lesson since the Vietnam era, when veterans of that war were treated very shabbily. And that is that if you don't like a war this country is involved in, hold the public officials who got us into that war accountable, not the men and women who are fighting it. Today, most Americans, whether they are progressive or conservative, understand that we must do everything we can to make sure that the men and women who put their lives on the line in service to this country get the quality health care and other benefits to which they are entitled.

Across this country, teachers are on the march. They are fighting for their students and they are fighting for their rights as workers. We all owe a deep debt of gratitude to the public school teachers in West Virginia, Kentucky, Oklahoma, Arizona, and Colorado who had the courage to go on strike and demand that education be adequately funded in their respective states. These teachers are a model for all of us who want to get our national priorities right.

In the richest nation on earth, we need to attract highly quali-fied people into the teaching profession, and we need to respect and adequately compensate them for the enormously important work they do. Educators in this country should not be working for inad-equate wages and benefits and should not be teaching in antiquated school buildings without state-of-the-art technology or up-to-date books.

If our government can provide a trillion dollars in tax breaks to the richest 1 percent and expand military spending by $165 billion over two years, we can surely provide high-quality public educa-tion from pre-K through college.

On Saturday afternoon, I spoke to several hundred Vermont teachers at a rally in Montpelier, our state capital, sponsored by the

Vermont chapter of the National Education Association (NEA). As in many other states, Vermont's public education system is under attack on a number of fronts. I was proud to stand with Vermont teachers in defense of high-quality public education in our state.

DOING THE SUNDAY NEWS SHOWS

This morning I was on *Meet the Press* with Chuck Todd. Last week, I did *State of the Union* with Jake Tapper.

For most of my political career I was rarely invited to be on the Sunday news shows. Since the presidential campaign of 2016, that has changed, and I am now a frequent guest. I have ambivalent feelings about these shows.

The positive, obviously, is that you get five to ten minutes on national television to speak directly to millions of people. That's no small thing, and it's a lot better than the usual seven-second sound bite that you get on TV news.

The negative is that national television has pretty strong limitations as to what can be discussed, and the issues that I care about most are often ignored on these programs.

Further, going on these shows exposes you to "gotcha" questions that then get picked up by the national media who report on the interview.

Overall, however, I think that the positives outweigh the negatives, and I accept most of the invitations I receive.

In preparing for these shows, my staff and I do our best to find out what subjects the host wants to cover and how we can best answer the questions we think will be asked. Sometimes, however, the issues we were told would be covered are completely ignored and are subsumed by the "news of the day." Maybe Trump sent out a tweet. Maybe there was a tragedy. Maybe someone said something really dumb. *Senator, what do you think?*

The interview with Chuck went well, and his questions were consistent with what NBC had told us they wanted to discuss. Mostly, we focused on the future of the Democratic Party. Chuck wanted to know if progressives could actually win elections or whether successful candidates had to be centrists.

I told Chuck what I have said many, many times. Progressive ideas are now mainstream in America. That's what the people want, especially Democrats. Further, a progressive agenda is not only good public policy; it is what winning campaigns are all about. Democrats usually do well when voter turnout is high. Republicans usually do well when voter turnout is low. In 2014, in the midterm elections, the United States had the lowest voter turnout since World War II. Republicans won landslide victories.

The only way that turnout goes up is when candidates speak to the needs of working people, lower-income people, and young people—people who are marginal voters. When there is political excitement in the air, when ordinary people sense hope for the future, they will come out and vote, and Democrats will win. The simple truth is that "moderates" or "centrists" do not generate that level of excitement.

Chuck also asked me about another school shooting, this one in Texas, that had claimed ten lives and had taken place a few days before. What, he asked, could be done? My answer was simple and straightforward. The American people, gun owners and non-gun owners, overwhelmingly support commonsense gun safety legislation. They want increased background checks, they want to end the gun show loophole, and they want other provisions that would make it harder for those people who should not own guns to have them. The problem: as I stated previously, Trump and almost all Republicans are scared to death of the NRA and are paralyzed into inaction. Until that changes, Congress will not pass any meaningful gun safety laws.

May 28, 2018

RUNNING FOR REELECTION
TO THE U.S. SENATE

Today, to nobody's great surprise, I announced my intention to seek reelection for a third term to the U.S. Senate. The state's filing deadline is May 31, and volunteers and staff had collected the necessary signatures from registered voters to get me on the ballot.

The decision was not a difficult one. Yes, I felt a bit envious of two close friends who had retired during the year. Phil Fiermonte, who had worked with me for decades, was traveling the country with his fiancée—taking in spring training games and golf in Florida, and skiing in Colorado. Huck Gutman, who had taught at the University of Vermont for forty-five years, now had more time to write, enjoy his extended family, and focus on the poetry that he loved.

As attractive as retirement might seem, Jane and I had concluded that it was just not conceivable for us to walk away from the enormous problems facing our state and nation—struggles that we were deeply immersed in and that affected our seven grandchildren and every kid in this country. It would not be possible for me to be an observer. I had to remain on the battlefield, in the midst of the political struggle.

What would this 2018 campaign look like? Impossible to say. Up to now, at least, no major Republican candidate had announced his or her intention to run for the seat. The fear remains, however, that as a result of *Citizens United*, any vaguely serious candidate running against me could attract millions of dollars from the Koch brothers, Wall Street, the pharmaceutical industry, and other powerful special interests I have taken on over the years. I am popular in the state and absolutely confident that I will win reelection. The only question is how brutal and negative the campaign could be.

I have run for office in Vermont as an Independent since my 1981 campaign for mayor of Burlington, and I am now the longest-serving Independent in congressional history. In Vermont, that is what I have always done, and what Vermonters expect me to do, and what I will always do. Meanwhile, in Washington, I have been a member of the Democratic Caucus in the House for the sixteen years I served there and a member of the Democratic Caucus in the Senate for the last twelve years. Today, of course, I am a member of the Democratic Senate Leadership team. All this creates a somewhat unusual dynamic for my election efforts in Vermont, a situation that is not fully understood by some national media and intentionally distorted by political opponents.

In Vermont, I am strongly supported by the Vermont Democratic Party and have helped lead the effort to get Vermont Democrats elected to office, including the state's last Democratic governor, the present lieutenant governor, and many members of the legislature. My campaign has made significant financial contributions to Vermont Democratic candidates, as well as large donations to the Vermont Democratic Party's coordinated campaigns. Given that reality, the state Democratic leadership and I agree that it would be absurd to have a Democrat run against me in the general election, split the vote, and open the possibility of a Republican winning.

How do we address this situation? It's not complicated. For my last two Senate races, I have run in the Democratic primary, won it, respectfully declined the nomination, and appeared on the ballot as an Independent. This is a strategy that works well for Vermont Democrats, for me, and for the state's progressive movement.

But to complicate matters further, we have the strongest progressive third party in the country, the Vermont Progressive Party. It grew out of the political movement that I helped lead when I was mayor of Burlington, and it has elected more candidates to the legislature than any other third party in America. I have been strongly supportive of the Progressive Party and its agenda and have done my best to see that Democrats and Progressives work together as closely as possible and do not act in a way that benefits Republicans.

When I announced that I would run for reelection to the Senate, the media's response, both in Vermont and nationally, included the question: Would I be running for president in 2020? My answer was that my focus now was on winning reelection to the Senate by running a strong grassroots campaign involving hundreds of volunteers who would be knocking on doors throughout the state. I was also going to do everything possible to help progressive candidates throughout the country win their contests in this all-important midterm election.

The year 2020 remains a long way off.

TAKING ON DISNEY

One of the largely untold stories in America is the incredible number of people who are struggling economically. And I'm not just talking about the elderly on fixed incomes, the children, or the disabled. I am talking about people who go to work every single day.

In the midst of a "strong" economy, and with unemployment relatively low, tens of millions of our people are still forced to work two or three jobs, six or seven days a week. In the midst of massive income and wealth inequality, these workers are unable to find affordable housing or child care. Many of them lack the income to pay for health insurance or prescription drugs, and most of them have little or nothing in the bank as they prepare for retirement.

While Republicans have been increasingly vicious in their attacks against working families, I have long been convinced that Democrats have been much too weak in taking on corporate power and standing up for employees. The rich get richer, the middle class gets poorer, and Democrats remain much too silent. Too many Democrats spend too much time raising money from the wealthy and corporate interests and too little time fighting for those who are being economically exploited. Come election time, Democrats ask workers for their support and continue to be surprised when these workers don't show up to vote or, even worse, vote Republican. The bottom line is that if you don't stand up for your constituents, they're not going to stand up for you.

On June 2, I went to Anaheim, California, home of Disneyland. I wasn't there to take my grandchildren to meet Donald Duck and Mickey Mouse or to go on the rides. I was there to attend a rally with over 1,500 Disney workers who were being ruthlessly exploited by Disney, an extremely wealthy and powerful multinational corporation. The rally was organized by a number of unions and held in a large church. A union organizer, Jennifer Muir Beuthin, whose grandparents had actually met when they worked at Disneyland many years before, opened the program and introduced me. I spoke for a few minutes and was followed by six current Disney workers who told us about their lives.

My remarks were straightforward. Disney is a $150 billion corporation and made $9 billion in profits in 2017. It received a $1.5 billion tax break from the Trump tax giveaway to the rich and, unsurprisingly, has received hundreds of millions in local tax breaks from the City of Anaheim. Further, I thought it ironic that, while paying its workers extremely low wages, the Disney board had recently reached a four-year compensation agreement with its CEO, Bob Iger, for an estimated $423 million.

And yet, while Disney's profits soared, and its CEO received an unimaginable amount of money, the wages and benefits for the workers at Disney were atrocious. The people who walked around all day in Mickey Mouse and Donald Duck costumes, the workers who prepared and delivered the food, the men and women who collected tickets and managed the rides made wages so low that they were barely surviving.

In October 2017, Occidental College issued a report on the economic condition of the workers at Disneyland. Anaheim is an expensive community in which to live. And yet, despite steep increases in the cost of housing and other necessities, Disneyland workers have suffered steady pay cuts, after adjusting for inflation.

The average hourly wage for Disneyland Resort workers in real dollars dropped 15 percent from 2000 to 2017, from $15.80 to $13.36. Today, over 80 percent of Disneyland workers make less than $15 an hour. Almost three-quarters say that they do not earn enough money to cover basic expenses every month. Over half of Disneyland employees report concerns about being evicted from their homes or apartments.

Incredibly, more than one out of ten Disneyland Resort employees report having been homeless (or not having a place of their own to sleep) in the past two years. More than two-thirds (68 percent) of Disneyland Resort workers are food-insecure. Only 28 percent report having the same schedule every week.

Reports and statistics are one thing. Hearing real human beings describe what's going on in their lives is another, and the testimony we heard from the six Disney employees was both heartbreaking and mind-blowing.

Glynndana Shevlin sat next to me onstage. The fifty-eight-year-old food and beverage worker and member of Unite HERE Local 11 has worked at Disneyland for thirty years. Over the past decade, she's seen her wages go up a whopping $2.

"I go hungry most days on one meal a day," she told the crowd, according to the *Washington Examiner*. "I work in the most beautiful room in the Adventure Tower at the Disneyland hotel. . . . I feed these guests the most amazing gourmet food you've ever seen that at the end of the day gets thrown in a recycle bin. If I eat that food or even try it[—]they call it separated from the company[,] like we're family—you're going to be shunned. They freakin' fire us if we eat one little crumb."

There's no moral defense for this. As I said that day, "Let me break the news to people watching: ducks don't talk, mice really don't talk. That's fantasy—this is reality. And the reality is that someone who has worked for an enormously successful and profitable corporation for thirty years should not be going hungry."

My appearance in Anaheim attracted the attention of the Disney Corporation. The day before I arrived, they made public an offer they had negotiated with the unions. I agreed with the unions that while the offer was a modest step forward, Disney had a very long way to go to meet the legitimate needs of its workers.

While I was there, Disneyland spokeswoman Suzi Brown issued the following statement: "We are proud of our commitment to our cast, and the fact that more people choose to work at Disneyland Resort than anywhere else in Orange County. While Mr. Sanders continues to criticize Disney to keep himself in the headlines, we continue to support our cast members through investments in wages and education." Hmmm. Attacking me rather than defending their employment policies tells me that they know they are in the wrong, big time.

Back in Washington, my staff produced social media video clips of the workers' testimony, which were viewed by millions of people. I will continue doing everything I can to work with the unions there in demanding decent wages, benefits, and working conditions at Disneyland. The bottom line is that if you work forty hours a week or more, you should not be living in poverty.

While in Southern California, I was able to observe that starvation wages were not unique to the workers in Disneyland. After we left Anaheim, we traveled to the Port of Los Angeles, where we participated in a rally with truck drivers organized by the

Teamsters. I was joined there by Congresswoman Nanette Diaz Barragán.

The issue here goes beyond the terrible wages and working conditions that these mostly Latino truck drivers receive. What they are up against is a growing practice in our economy of employers engaging in illegal wage theft and the misclassification of their employees.

In the case of these workers, in order for them to get a truck-driving job they had to sign on as "independent contractors" and were forced to lease the trucks they were driving for an outrageously high fee. The result: After paying all of the insurance, fuel, maintenance, and other costs associated with leasing a truck, one driver told me that he worked one hundred hours one week, and not only did he not get paid, but he ended up owing the company a check. Other drivers talked about working seven days a week and sleeping in their trucks.

As independent contractors, these workers receive no guaranteed minimum wage, no overtime pay, and no health care or retirement benefits, and they have to pay 100 percent of their Social Security and Medicare payroll taxes. In many ways, not only are they ruthlessly exploited, but they exist as modern-day indentured servants. They work incredibly hard but often go further and further into debt.

I am proud to have recently introduced legislation to stop companies from misclassifying workers as independent contractors and to make it easier for workers to form unions. Sixteen of my Senate colleagues have cosponsored that bill.

My last public event of the day in Southern California was a wonderful and unique experience. Along with some of the leading criminal justice advocates in the country—Shaun King, Patrisse Cullors, Ivette Ale, Melina Abdullah, Jayda Rasberry, and Jasmyne Cannick—we held a rally, actually two rallies, calling for fundamental reform of our broken criminal justice system. The event was held at the Million Dollar Theatre, the oldest movie house in Los Angeles, which seats 2,300 people. The reason we held two rallies was that we had a large overflow crowd, and before we began the event in the theater, we had to go outside and address the thousand people who were unable to get in.

The size of the crowd told me something very important. And that was that criminal justice was no longer a fringe issue, supported by Black Lives Matter and a handful of other grassroots organizations. Because of the tireless work of the people who were up on the stage with me, people who had devoted their entire lives to the struggle, criminal justice was an issue that was now prime time and was finally getting the attention it deserved.

Shaun King, who had helped organize the event, had a really brilliant idea. He was trying to redefine the function of a district attorney or a prosecutor. He talked about Real Justice PAC, an organization he had cofounded, which was helping elect progressive district attorneys and prosecutors across the country. This organization was supporting candidates who were not about simply locking up more and more people. Instead, they were trying to address the real causes of crime and to lower the jail population.

Patrisse Cullors is an artist and organizer and a cofounder of Black Lives Matter. She talked about her efforts to stop a $3.5 billion jail expansion plan in Los Angeles County. In this effort, she couldn't be more right. Think about it for a moment. Schools and job-training programs around the country are underfunded, and we have millions of kids leaving school completely unprepared to find jobs in today's complex economy. Somehow, we have billions of dollars available for more jails and incarceration, but we can't afford to provide these kids with the education they need to survive in modern America. That doesn't make a lot of sense to me.

I was honored to be up on a stage with these heroes and heroines and will continue working with them in the months and years to come. Let us end the international embarrassment of the United States having more people in jail than any other country. Instead, let's fight to make this country the best educated on the planet.

June 26, 2018

A GOOD ELECTION NIGHT

On June 24, 2018, the *New York Times* ran a front-page story headlined "Bernie Sanders Is Winning Converts: But Primary Victories Remain Elusive." The essence of the piece was that while my ideas were catching on, my political influence and the impact of Our Revolution was not electorally significant. The *Times* was picking up on a media narrative that had been developed a month before, pushed by establishment Democrats, that candidates who supported a progressive agenda just couldn't win elections. The implication: the only political path forward for the Democratic Party was centrist politics, the same old same old.

In their story, the *Times* covered a rally that I did with my good friend Ben Jealous, who was running for the Democratic nomination for governor of Maryland. Ben, a strong progressive and the former president of the national NAACP, had been an active surrogate for me during my presidential campaign, and I was involved in his gubernatorial campaign from the very beginning.

Ben started his campaign relatively unknown in Maryland and way behind in the polls. But because of a bold progressive message and a strong grassroots effort, he was now tied for the lead, and I was proud to join him for our fourth rally together, an outdoor event in Silver Spring on a hot and humid night.

The *Times* coverage, though, focused not on what the large turn-out at the rally might mean for Ben's campaign, nor what Ben or I or any other speaker said, but instead on what Ben's campaign meant in terms of my political influence. They wrote:

> *The race in Maryland has also become a critical test of Mr. Sanders's ability to sway elections. If his policy agenda has caught on widely among Democratic candidates, and succeeded in moving the party to the left, Mr. Sanders himself has struggled so far to expand his political base and propel his personal allies to victory in Democratic primaries.*
>
> *He has endorsed only a handful of candidates in contested primaries, and three of them have recently lost difficult races in Iowa and Pennsylvania.*
>
> *In addition, an advocacy organization aligned with Mr. Sanders, Our Revolution, has had only marginal success. Though it has touted its electoral victories in recent primaries, fewer than 50 percent of the more than 80 candidates it has endorsed have won elections this year.*

The *Times* story, as is often the case with mainstream coverage of progressive politics, missed the main point.

It is not difficult to endorse candidates who win 100 percent of the time. Just support candidates who are ahead in the polls, have a lot of money, and enjoy establishment support. That is precisely what we do not do. We support candidates, sometimes major long-shot candidates, who are prepared to take on the economic and political establishment and run strong grassroots campaigns.

Ben Jealous's campaign in the Maryland Democratic gubernatorial primary reminded me very much of my own presidential campaign. He had started way behind, was taking on virtually the entire Democratic establishment, and was running an aggressive campaign that was bringing thousands of young people into the political process. His opponent, Rushern Baker, was a moderate Democrat who had the support of a Maryland senator, a powerful Maryland congressman, former Maryland governors, and most members of the state legislature.

By 10:00 p.m. the election results were coming in, and Ben was doing well all across the state, far better than we had ever hoped. He was winning big in black districts in Baltimore and more than holding his own elsewhere. By the end of the evening, it was clear that he had won an enormous victory. In a nine-person race, he had received almost 40 percent of the vote and had won by more than 58,000 votes.

Ben's primary win in Maryland was not the only important progressive victory of the night.

In New York City, a twenty-eight-year-old first-time candidate pulled off a major, major upset by defeating one of the most powerful members of Congress in a Democratic congressional primary race.

Alexandria Ocasio-Cortez, a member of the Democratic Socialists of America and an organizer in my presidential campaign, defeated Congressman Joe Crowley by 15 points. Alexandria, who a year before had been waiting tables at a bar, ran on a strongly progressive agenda, as Ben had done. She was fighting for Medicare for All, free tuition at public colleges and universities, vigorous opposition to Trump's inhumane immigration policies, and a $15-an-hour minimum wage.

No doubt the *New York Times* was disappointed. It turns out that not only were progressive ideas catching on all across the country, but our candidates were also pulling off major upsets and winning elections.

The bottom line, as I have always believed, is that if a strong candidate runs on issues that make sense to working people and puts together a large and motivated volunteer base, that candidate can win elections. That's what Ben and Alexandria did in Maryland and New York City. That's what can happen anywhere in the country. And that's what the political revolution is all about.

July 11, 2018

THE SUPREME COURT MATTERS

On July 9, President Trump nominated Brett Kavanaugh for a lifetime seat on the U.S. Supreme Court to replace retiring justice Anthony Kennedy. This is a nomination I will vigorously oppose.

Many Americans have a pretty good idea of what Congress does. They have a pretty good sense of what the president does. But they do not, in my view, have a clear understanding of what the Supreme Court does, much less the enormous importance it has for everyday life.

In the past decade, a right-wing Supreme Court has issued some incredibly destructive decisions, often by a 5–4 vote, that have had a profound impact upon every man, woman, and child in America. Just a few examples:

The Supreme Court has helped create a corrupt campaign finance system that substantially benefits the rich and the powerful against the needs of working people. Whether you are a progressive or a conservative or somewhere in between, you know that there is something profoundly wrong when a small number of billionaires can spend many hundreds of millions of dollars to try to buy elections. That is not what American democracy is supposed to be about, and the American people know it.

What most Americans don't know, however, is that this situation was created by a 5–4 Supreme Court vote in the *Citizens United* case of 2010, which struck down parts of the comprehensive bipartisan campaign finance legislation that Congress had passed. That decision paved the way for corporations and billionaires to spend unlimited sums of money on political campaigns and undermine the foundations of American democracy.

The Supreme Court has helped deny millions of lower-income Americans the health care they desperately need. Today in America, millions of low-income working people have no health insurance and are unable to go to the doctor when they get sick. Thousands of these people die every year from illnesses that could have been treated if they had insurance. And that is why Congress passed the Affordable Care Act, which, among other provisions, expanded the Medicaid program to make sure that all low-income people had access to health insurance.

In 2012, the constitutionality of that legislation was challenged by a conservative business group. While the Court upheld the constitutionality of the Affordable Care Act, it ruled, by a 5–4 vote, that the important provision expanding Medicaid could be optional for states. The result: seventeen states have still not expanded Medicaid, leaving millions of the poorest people in our country without health insurance. As a member of the committee that helped write the ACA, I can assure you we never intended that provision to be optional.

The Supreme Court has made it easier for states, once again, to discriminate against people of color in terms of voting. Very few would deny that this country, going back to the days of slavery, has a shameful history on civil rights. It took the efforts of Dr. Martin

Luther King Jr. and millions of Americans in the civil rights movement to finally win the struggle to guarantee that all Americans, regardless of the color of their skin, had the right to vote. The key legislation enforcing that right was the 1965 Voting Rights Act, legislation that was reauthorized multiple times.

In 2013, in *Shelby County v. Holder*, by a 5–4 vote, the Supreme Court claimed that major parts of the Voting Rights Act were outdated and struck them down. This decision opened the floodgates for a massive campaign of voter suppression, as Republican state officials immediately began to enact voter restrictions targeted at black people, poor people, young people, and other groups who don't traditionally vote for them.

More recently, again by a 5–4 vote, the Court enshrined religious discrimination in our travel and immigration policies by upholding Trump's Muslim ban. And, in the *Janus* case, they ruled that unions could not collect fees from non-union employees who benefited from union-negotiated contracts—one of the most anti-union decisions in modern history. The corporate world brought that case to the Court as part of their effort to weaken unions like AFSCME and teachers' unions, which are an important part of the progressive coalition in this country.

Right now, as the above decisions make clear, the Supreme Court has a 5–4 conservative majority that regularly rules on behalf of right-wing partisan and wealthy corporate interests. But the court is not as conservative as Trump and the Republican leadership would like. After Mitch McConnell blocked the confirmation process on Obama nominee Merrick Garland for nearly a year, Trump appointed one extreme right-wing justice, Neil Gorsuch, and now they want another.

On some issues, the retiring Justice Kennedy has cast a swing vote, aligning himself with the liberal minority. Most noteworthy, he has voted to protect a woman's right to choose, and he wrote the majority decision in *Obergefell v. Hodges*, the case that protected gay people's right to marry.

On July 11, I went to the floor of the Senate to oppose Brett Kavanaugh's nomination to the Supreme Court. This is some of what I said:

> [While] I do not usually believe what President Trump says, this is one of those rare times when I think we should take him at his word. During the campaign, he was asked if he wanted to see the Court overturn *Roe v. Wade* and he said, "Well, if we put another two or perhaps three justices on, that's really what's going to be—that will happen. And that'll happen automatically, in my opinion, because I am putting pro-life justices on the court."
>
> On a separate occasion, he suggested women who have abortions should be punished.
>
> And as we all know, he put forth a list of twenty-five potential justices, handpicked by the Heritage Foundation and the Federalist Society. These two extreme right-wing groups claim that they have "no idea" how any of the people on that list would rule on *Roe v. Wade*, but overruling *Roe* has been a Republican dream for forty years. Please do not insult our intelligence by suggesting that it's possible any of these candidates may secretly support a woman's right to control her own body.
>
> So that brings us to Judge Kavanaugh. You may remember last year the federal government was sued by an undocumented teenage girl they were keeping in detention in Texas. She discovered she was pregnant while in detention and tried to obtain an abortion. Judge Kavanaugh wanted to

force her to delay the proceeding—presumably until it was no longer legal under Texas law for her to obtain an abortion in the state. When he was overruled by the full DC Circuit, he complained in a dissent that his colleagues were creating a right to "abortion on demand." Does that sound like someone who is going to strike down state laws that create undue barriers to abortion access? Or does it sound like someone who had no problem with forcing a teenage girl to carry a pregnancy to term?

There is also another case percolating out of Texas which could have even graver consequences for millions of Americans. Texas and seventeen other Republican states have sued the government, claiming the Affordable Care Act is unconstitutional—and the Department of Justice agrees with them! Now, while I do not know how Judge Kavanaugh would rule on this case, I will note that in another case about the ACA, he suggested that the president could simply refuse to enforce laws that he deems unconstitutional, regardless of what the courts say. So we have a scenario where the Department of Justice argues it is unconstitutional to prevent insurance companies from discriminating against people with preexisting conditions, and according to Judge Kavanaugh's own writing, they could possibly stop enforcing that provision?

We do not even need to speculate about how he would rule as a justice of the Supreme Court. We can look at how he has ruled as a judge on the DC Circuit.

Time and time again, Judge Kavanaugh has sided with the interests of corporations and millionaires and billionaires instead of with the interests of the American people. He has sided with electric power utilities and chemical companies over protecting clean air and fighting climate change. He argued that the Consumer Financial Protection Bureau was unconstitutional because its structure did not give enough power to the president. He argued against net neutrality. He dissented in an Occupational Safety and Health Administration case, arguing that Sea World should not be fined for the death of one of its whale trainers because the trainer should have accepted the risk of death as a routine part of the job.

So while we cannot predict the future, we can see the record Judge Kavanaugh has set and extrapolate from that the kinds of decisions we expect him to make if he is confirmed as a Supreme Court justice. I cannot say with any confidence that a Justice Kavanaugh would side with the American people.

My hope for those of us who believe in a woman's right to choose, who believe that LGBT Americans should not have to face discrimination, who believe in the right to vote, who believe that health care is a right, not a privilege, is that we can defeat this nomination, and that President Trump will send the Senate a nominee who can garner overwhelming bipartisan support.

Do I believe that we can defeat Trump's nomination of Kavanaugh to the Supreme Court? Clearly, the odds are against us, and it will be a very difficult fight. Right now, there are 51 Republicans in the Senate and 49 members of the Democratic Caucus. In order to defeat Kavanaugh, we would have to hold on to every Democrat and win one or two Republicans—depending upon whether John McCain, who is battling cancer, would return to vote.

Up to now, the Republicans have been unified on judicial votes, including the votes for Gorsuch.

On the other hand, there are two Republican senators, Lisa Murkowski and Susan Collins, who are pro-choice. Will they support a nominee who in all likelihood will strike down *Roe v. Wade*? Colorado is a strong pro-choice state. Will the Republican senator there, Cory Gardner, vote against the desires of his constituents?

Judge Kavanaugh has written that a president should be able to "deem" laws unconstitutional and not enforce them, even if a court has found the law constitutional. Wow! That's a pretty radical statement in terms of executive authority and against the separation of powers. Can libertarian-type senators like Rand Paul and Mike Lee be comfortable with those views?

The bottom line is that this is an enormously important nomination. Kavanaugh's lifetime appointment to the Supreme Court will create a hard-right conservative majority for years to come, and will be a disaster for the country.

The American people must understand the significance of this nomination and become involved in the debate. And I intend to play an active role in that process.

TRUMP EMBARRASSES AMERICA (AGAIN)

On July 16, President Trump met in Helsinki with Russian president Vladimir Putin. It was a disaster, and an embarrassment for the American people.

For well over a year now, every U.S. intelligence agency that studied the issue has made it abundantly clear that Russia interfered in the 2016 presidential election on behalf of Donald Trump and against Hillary Clinton. In a rare showing of bipartisanship, the intelligence committees of the U.S. House and the U.S. Senate reached that same conclusion, as did the entire Senate and the House. Just a few days before the Trump-Putin meeting, Special Counsel Robert Mueller announced a set of indictments of twelve members of Russia's military intelligence service, the GRU, for their involvement in the election. This follows other indictments against Russian nationals issued months before.

Speaking at an event on July 13, a few days before the Helsinki summit, Dan Coats, a former Republican senator and now director of national intelligence, raised the alarm on growing cyberattack threats against the United States in a range of areas, including federal, state, and local government agencies, the military, business, and academia, saying that the situation was at a "critical point." He said Russia is the "most aggressive foreign actor, no question. And they continue their efforts to undermine our democracy." Coats compared the warning signs to those the United States faced ahead of the September 11 terrorist attacks.

In other words, the debate over Russian interference in our 2016 election, as well as their meddling in the elections of many other democracies around the world, has long been over. Everybody is in agreement—except Donald Trump.

The *New York Times* reported that Trump was shown highly classified intelligence two weeks before his inauguration that indicated that Putin had personally ordered complex cyberattacks to sway the election. Nonetheless, when asked at a press conference in Helsinki whether he believed the Russians had tried to influence the election, he replied, "[Putin] just said it's not Russia. I will say this. I don't see any reason why it would be."

The day after his press conference, after a strong international backlash, Trump, in a bizarre statement, claimed he misspoke and of course blamed the media for reporting what he had said instead of what he had meant: "wouldn't" instead of "would." Even then he could not help but suggest that the electoral interference "could be other people also," and not just Russia.

The late senator John McCain, someone I did not often agree with, was right when he wrote that the Helsinki summit was "one of the most disgraceful performances by an American president in memory. The damage inflicted by President Trump's naivete, egotism, false equivalence, and sympathy for autocrats is difficult to calculate. But it is clear that the summit in Helsinki was a tragic mistake."

On July 17, I went to the floor and remarked:

My friends, today we face an unprecedented situation of a
president who for whatever reason refuses to acknowledge the
full scope of the threat to American democracy: Either he
really doesn't understand what has happened, or he is under
Russian influence because of compromising information
they may have on him, or because he is ultimately more
sympathetic to Russia's authoritarian-oligarchic form of
government than he is to American democracy.

Whatever the reason, Congress must act, and act now, to
demand that the president of the United States represent the
interests of the American people and not Russia.

What is increasingly apparent, and extremely distressing, is the
degree to which a frightened Republican majority in Congress has
abdicated its responsibility in maintaining an independent branch
of government. Their fear of Trump and "his base" prevents them
from opposing the president on almost any issue, even when he em-
barrasses the country and undermines fundamental American values. This goes beyond a Democrat-Republican debate. This is about
our constitutional form of government, and the role that Congress
must play.

At the Democratic Caucus on July 17, I spoke about the need
to force Republicans to act on this matter, and my intention to bring
forth a "sense of the Senate" resolution reaffirming our outrage at
the president's behavior and in support of strong action against
Russian interference in our elections and other aspects of our society. On July 19, Chuck Schumer and I went to the floor and presented a resolution that called for a course of action containing the
following directives:

1. The Congress must make it clear that we accept the assessment of our intelligence community with regard to Russian election interfering in our country and in other democracies.

2. The Congress must move aggressively to protect our election systems from interference by Russia or any foreign power, and work closely with our democratic partners around the world to do the same.

3. The Congress must demand that the sanctions against Russia passed last year be fully implemented.

4. The Congress must make it clear that we will not accept any interference with the ongoing investigation of Special Counsel Mueller, such as the offer of preemptive pardons or the firing of Deputy Attorney General Rod Rosenstein, and that the president must cooperate with this investigation.

5. The Congress must make it clear to President Trump that his job is to protect the values that millions of Americans struggled, fought, and died to defend: democracy, justice, and equality.

Tweets, comments, and press conferences are fine, but we need more from Republican senators now. It's time for the Senate to rein in the president's dangerous behavior. If their leadership won't allow votes on this extraordinarily important matter, then my Republican colleagues must join with Democrats to make it happen, or all of their words are worthless.

Sadly, but not surprisingly, the frightened Republican leadership objected to my "unanimous consent" and refused to allow the resolution to come up for a debate and a vote. Taking on the president is not something they want to do, no matter how absurd or dangerous his behavior is.

WHICH WAY FORWARD?

Here are two media stories, written a day apart, that pretty much lay out the choices we face regarding the future of the Democratic Party and politics in America.

July 20, 2018, the *Wichita Eagle*:

BERNIE SANDERS FIRES UP 4,000 IN WICHITA WITH RALLY FOR JAMES THOMPSON, AGAINST TRUMP

With the gruff and at times angry rhetoric that made him famous on the campaign trail, former Democratic presidential candidate Bernie Sanders fired up a crowd of about 4,000 on Friday with a speech calling on Kansans to support progressive ideals and a local Democrat for Congress.

Sanders and Democratic rising star Alexandria Ocasio-Cortez came to Wichita to rally on behalf of James Thompson, running for Kansas' 4th Congressional District seat.

The article concludes:

Guadalupe Magdaleno, executive director of Sunflower Community Action, said she came to the rally because she was tired of divisive rhetoric against the immigrant community.

"When we see that hate is being spread in our nation and dividing our communities by our color, by our gender, by our religion or by where we're from, a rally like this brings us hope," she said. "All around the rally, you saw people from all different backgrounds, showing that we're a progressive and just nation. This rally lifted our spirits, brought us hope and encourages us to continue the fight."

Here is the other article:

July 21, NBC News

Sanders' wing of the party terrifies moderate Dems. Here's how they plan to stop it. Party members and fundraisers gathered for an invitation-only event to figure out how to counteract the rising progressive movement.

COLUMBUS, Ohio—If Bernie Sanders is leading a leftist political revolt, then a summit here of moderate Democrats might be the start of a counterrevolution.

While the energy and momentum is with progressives these days—the victory of rising star Alexandria Ocasio-Cortez in New York, buzz about Democratic Socialism and the spread of the "Abolish ICE!" movement are a few recent examples— moderates are warning that ignoring them will lead the party to disaster in the midterm elections and the 2020 presidential contest.

That anxiety has largely been kept to a whisper among the party's moderates and big donors, with some of the major fundraisers pressing operatives on what can be done to stop the Vermonter if he runs for the White House again.

The article continues:

The gathering here was just that—an effort to offer an attractive alternative to the rising Sanders-style populist left in the upcoming presidential race. Where progressives see a rare opportunity to capitalize on an energized Democratic base, moderates see a better chance to win over Republicans turned off by Trump.

The fact that a billionaire real estate developer, Winston Fisher, co-hosted the event and addressed attendees twice underscored that this group is not interested in the class warfare vilifying the "millionaires and billionaires" found in Sanders' stump speech.

So there it is. The choice is clear. Either we get new people involved in the political process by fighting for an agenda that represents the needs of working people—white, black, Latino, Asian American, and Native American—or we raise money from billionaires, support a corporate agenda, and hope that some Republicans disgusted with Trump will vote Democratic.

The victory of Alexandria Ocasio-Cortez makes it very clear to me which direction we should move in. Two years ago, she was a campaign coordinator for my presidential campaign in the Bronx. A year ago she was a twenty-seven-year-old waitress working in a bar. Last month, as a first-time candidate, she defeated one of the most powerful Democrats in Congress, Joe Crowley.

In winning the primary, Alexandria did all the right things. In addition to her progressive agenda, she understood that no one person can do it alone. Instead of relying on consultants and pollsters, she put together a strong, energized volunteer network that helped her knock on doors and get the word out. It turned out that Crowley's 5–1 spending advantage mattered very little when confronted with grassroots activism.

"We meet a machine with a movement, and that is what we have done today," Ocasio-Cortez told NY1 before the race was called. "I think what we've seen is that working-class Americans want a clear champion and there is nothing radical about moral clarity in 2018."

On Friday, July 20, Alexandria and I campaigned for two Democratic congressional candidates in Kansas, James Thompson and Brent Welder. Kansas? Why, you ask, would we go to Kansas, one of the most conservative states in the country, where Republicans control virtually all levels of government? Kansas is a state where Trump won by 21 points.

Well, here's the answer: The Democratic Party will never succeed if it continues to concede half the states in the country to right-wing Republicans. It cannot be a party of the East Coast, the West Coast, and a few states in between. It must be a fifty-state party, and, last I heard, Kansas was one of those states. Besides, there were two strong progressive candidates running good campaigns who, because of their hard work, had a shot to win.

I had briefly talked to Alexandria the day after she won her primary but met her for the first time at breakfast in Wichita. After comparing notes about how we could best work together at a joint appearance on CBS's *Face the Nation*, which would take place in an hour, we ventured over to the rally.

And what an enormous success that was. The turnout of 4,000

on a Friday afternoon was far larger than anyone expected, and full of energy. It was a crowd of all ages and backgrounds, people anxious to hear a progressive message in a sea of conservatism. This was an audience prepared to stand up and fight back.

After Alexandria and James spoke, it was my turn. In my prepared remarks, I thanked the people of Kansas for the landslide victory they gave me in the 2016 presidential primary and explained how their support had helped bring the progressive agenda into the mainstream.

I then told the people of Wichita why I was there.

I am here today because I believe that working families throughout our country are sick and tired of a rigged economy in which the very rich get richer while tens of millions of working families in Vermont, in the Bronx, and in Kansas struggle to make ends meet. No matter what part of the country you are in, people understand that there is something profoundly wrong when the three wealthiest people in this country own more wealth than the bottom half of America.

People from coast to coast are also disgusted with a corrupt campaign finance system in which billionaires, like your very own neighbors here in Wichita, the Koch brothers, are able to spend hundreds of millions of dollars to help elect candidates who represent the wealthy and the powerful.

And later I stated:

I have been asked in recent days why I wanted to come to Wichita and, later today, to Kansas City. Don't I know that this is a Republican state in which Donald Trump won a landslide victory? Yes. I know that. Don't I know that the governor is Republican, that the state legislature is Republican, and that your two senators are Republican? Yes. I know that too.

But this is what I also know. And that is that the differences that separate us, whether we live on the East Coast, the West Coast, or the Midwest, is no way as profound as that which binds us together as Americans and as human beings.

The truth is that there is a common humanity that unites all of us, whether we come from Vermont or Kansas, New York or Mississippi, or whether we are black or white, Latino, Native American or Asian American; whether we are men or women, gay or straight. No matter who we are the differences between us pale in comparison to what we all have in common.

Alexandria's mother came from Puerto Rico. My father came from Poland without a nickel in his pocket, and not speaking a word of English. Some of your families may have come from Germany or Ireland. But no matter where we come from or what our differences may be, the common humanity we share is that we all want our kids to have a good education. We all want decent jobs. We all want high-quality health care. We all want a secure retirement. We all want a clean environment. We all want a just society.

Our common humanity as human beings far outweighs any superficial differences we may have.

After the rally in Wichita, Alexandria and I, along with staff, drove three hours to Kansas City. In Vermont, our cows are mostly on small dairy farms. In Kansas, their beef cattle graze on large, flat ranges. It was quite a sight to behold from the window of our car.

In Kansas City, we more or less repeated what we had done in Wichita. This time, we were supporting Brent Welder. Once again, the turnout, 3,000, was far more than had been anticipated, and once again, there was an enormous amount of excitement.

Will James Thompson and Brent Welder win their Democratic primary races in August and go on to win their congressional elections in November? I don't know. Will Kansas in 2018 become a more progressive state? I don't know that, either. But this I do know with absolute certainty: if we don't start competing vigorously in Kansas, in Mississippi, in Wyoming, in Georgia, in Oklahoma, and in many other red states, if we don't provide the people there with a progressive alternative, we will never turn them around.

This was a great trip.

A STEP FORWARD FOR ECONOMIC JUSTICE

Today, by a 3–1 margin, union workers at Disneyland voted to approve a new contract that their leadership negotiated. This agreement, following months of strong worker protest, will lift the minimum wage at the theme park from $11 an hour to $13.25 an hour immediately, to $15 an hour on January 1, 2019, and up to $15.45 in June of 2020. As a result of this new contract, many of the lowest-paid workers there will be seeing annual salary increases of $8,000 a year. This may not be enough, but it is a good step forward in the fight for economic justice.

As Artemis Bell, a night-shift custodian and member of the bargaining committee, said after the contract was approved, "It's important for Disney, as the largest employer in Orange County, to recognize the struggles workers go through as the cost of living continues to rise in the area. . . . With this contract, we are one step closer to a better situation for thousands of employees who put so much energy and heart into their jobs."

As I wrote about earlier, I attended a rally in Anaheim eight weeks ago with several thousand Disney workers and, a few weeks later, invited one of the union negotiators to join me on a nationally televised town hall meeting with low-wage workers at other companies. Our social media also paid a lot of attention to the plight of the workers at Disneyland.

The situation at Disney reflects one of the great economic crises facing this country. In a nation where unemployment today is reasonably low, many millions of workers remain employed at wages that are simply unlivable. When you earn $9, $10, or $11 an hour, you just can't afford housing, health care, child care, transportation, decent food, or other basic necessities of life. This should not be happening in the wealthiest country in the history of the world, which is why I introduced legislation last year to raise the national minimum wage to $15 an hour.

In the meantime, while political support for that minimum-wage bill continues to grow, we have to continue to confront the major corporations, many of them extremely profitable, who pay their employees inadequate wages. And it's not just Disney. It's Walmart, it's McDonald's, it's American Airlines, and many, many other companies. It's Amazon, owned by Jeff Bezos, who, at this writing, is worth over $150 billion, the wealthiest person on earth. You tell me: Why should the taxpayers of this country spend billions a year subsidizing Mr. Bezos when many of his employees receive wages so low that they are forced to go on food stamps, Medicaid, or other federal programs?

The courage of the workers at Disneyland will not only benefit the employees there. Their struggle will send a message around the country that when workers stand together and fight for justice, they can win. Their success will encourage other workers to stand up and fight back.

On August 24, union workers also negotiated a minimum wage of $15 at Disney World, in Orlando, Florida—a significant increase.

Thank you, Disney employees.

REFORMING THE DEMOCRATIC PARTY

During the 2016 Democratic presidential primary, it became clear to me and to millions of Americans that the elitist, top-down approach of the party needed to be reformed. All over the country, people were demanding a Democratic Party that represented ordinary Americans and that allowed them to participate fully in the political process.

Clearly that was not happening, and the results were apparent. As a result of mass political disillusionment, the voter turnout in 2014 was historically low, and Republicans won landslide victories all across the country. By 2016, the Democrats had lost control of the White House, the U.S. Senate, and the U.S. House, and they had lost 1,000 seats in state legislatures. The operating business model of the Democratic Party was broken, and no sane person could defend it.

A clear manifestation of the top-down nature of the Democratic Party had everything to do with the role of superdelegates. The Democratic National Committee, in its wisdom, had designated 716 political insiders as superdelegates—delegates to the national convention who could support any candidate they wanted, regardless of how the people of their state had voted in their primaries or caucuses.

In other words, the Democratic leadership had created the absurd and undemocratic situation that allowed 30 percent of the votes needed for the presidential nomination to come from the party elite. In 2016, this grossly unfair situation became very apparent when Secretary Clinton received the support of some 500 superdelegates *before* the first popular vote was cast in the Iowa caucuses. The presidential primary contest was almost over before it had begun. What kind of message does that send to ordinary Americans about democracy and citizen participation?

That is why, at the end of the 2016 primary process, I urged Secretary Clinton to work with me to form a Unity Reform Commission. This body would address the problem of superdelegates as well as other issues that would make the party more open and democratic. Secretary Clinton agreed.

Secretary Clinton; the newly elected chair of the party, Tom Perez; and I each appointed members to the commission. My appointees were a group of strong progressive activists who represented different elements of the party. They included former CWA president Larry Cohen, as the co-chair of the body; my campaign manager, Jeff Weaver; former Ohio state senator and future Our Revolution president Nina Turner; former Nevada assemblywoman Lucy Flores; Jane Kleeb, chair of the Nebraska Democratic Party; activist Nomiki Konst; Jim Zogby, president of the Arab American Institute; and former Berkeley mayor Gus Newport. Hillary Clinton appointed a number of experienced and knowledgeable Democrats, as did Tom Perez.

The Unity Reform Commission held four public meetings around the country throughout the summer and fall of 2017.

Finally, in December of 2017, the group unanimously passed a resolution that would significantly reduce the power of superdelegates, open up primaries, reform caucuses, and make the internal workings of the party more transparent.

In the Twitter universe, the issue of Democratic Party reform generated an enormous amount of interest and conflict. But on the commission, there was a surprising degree of unanimity among the representatives from the Clinton, Sanders, and Perez camps. Each group had come to the conclusion that party reform was a necessity, and we worked effectively to bring it about.

The next step was to take the recommendations to the Rules and Bylaws Committee of the DNC. This committee, after several months both over the phone and in person, passed an even stronger version of superdelegate reform, completely eliminating any impact these party insiders can have on the first ballot at the convention.

These proposals were then sent on to the nearly 500 members of the Democratic National Committee.

Finally, on August 25, 2018, at a meeting in Chicago more than two years after the convention in Philadelphia, the full Democratic National Committee approved these changes by a voice vote. A headline on NBC News read, "Tom Perez and Bernie Sanders Teamed Up to Push the Biggest Reform Package the Party Has Seen in Decades."

Explaining the significance of the moment, Dave Weigel, of the *Washington Post*, wrote, "The new party rules undo decades-old reforms that empowered hundreds of party activists and elected officials, often referred to as 'superdelegates,' whose presidential convention votes were not bound to the results of primaries or caucuses."

In my view, these rule changes are an important first step in making the Democratic Party an institution that lives up to its democratic ideals. Not only is this the right thing to do, but it makes sense politically. Only a party that welcomes ordinary people into the process and stands up and fights for their rights will generate excitement and energy—and win elections.

That begins with the manner in which the party chooses to select its candidates and its leaders. Making the process as open and transparent as possible and making sure that voters know their choice will be the deciding factor is critical to its success.

Of course, there is much more work to be done. Our goal must be, to quote Abraham Lincoln at Gettysburg, to create a political party "of the people, by the people, for the people."

And that is what I want the Democratic Party to become.

WHERE WE GO FROM HERE

During the last two years, I have traveled to thirty-two states and spoken to tens of thousands of people. My goal has been to bring the American people together to fight for a government that represents all of us and not just a handful of billionaire campaign contributors. There have been ups and downs in this struggle, but few can deny that the progressive movement is making enormous progress.

The political revolution is about thinking big. It's not about one election, one candidate, one issue. It's about creating a movement that will transform the economic, political, social, and environmental life of our country. That is not easy, but it's what has to be done.

Over the last two years, progressives have made great progress in advancing the two key elements of the political revolution. First, the ideas that we have proposed, once considered "extreme" and "unrealistic," are now widely supported by the American people. Given a chance to be heard and debated, these proposals have become part of mainstream consciousness. Some of them, in fact, are already being implemented.

Second, more and more people, often young and working class, are engaging in the political struggle. They are marching in the streets. They are working on social media. They are becoming active in unions and other grassroots organizations. They are knocking on doors in support of progressive candidates. They are running for office, often for the very first time. They are standing up and fighting back.

Much has been accomplished. Much more, however, remains to be done.

On May 26, 2015, in Burlington, Vermont, I announced my intention to run for president and brought forth much of the progressive agenda that I intended to run on. Many of these ideas were unfamiliar to most Americans and sounded extreme. They were rejected out of hand not only by my opponent but by almost every editorial board in the country and virtually the entire political and economic establishment.

Then a funny thing happened. As my supporters and I traveled the country speaking to larger and larger crowds, these "unrealistic" positions that we advocated began sounding more and more realistic.

And ordinary Americans began searching for answers to questions that they were starting to think about.

Why, in the wealthiest country in the history of the world, do we have a massive level of income and wealth inequality? Why are millions of us forced to work two or three jobs because we earn starvation wages? Why, at a time of record-breaking profits, does the federal minimum wage remain an unlivable $7.25 per hour? Why do we continue to have trade policies that benefit the rich and large corporations at the expense of average workers?

Three years ago, a few brave Democrats in the Senate were advocating for a $12 federal minimum wage. Today, a majority of

Americans support a $15-an-hour minimum wage, and we have thirty cosponsors on my legislation that will put that into effect. All across the country, cities and states are passing $15-an-hour minimum-wage legislation.

We are making progress in creating a more just economy.

And by the way, when we talk about a fair wage, we cannot forget that women still earn some 80 cents on the dollar compared with men. There is overwhelming support in this country for pay equity—equal pay for equal work—and that is the right thing to do. Every man in this country must stand with the women to win that fight.

Three years ago, in the midst of the loud and contentious debate over the Affordable Care Act, there was virtually no discussion in this country about the need for universal health care and a Medicare for All, single-payer system. "Too radical, too expensive, unthinkable, the American people don't want it," shouted the critics.

Today, the American people understand that there is something fundamentally wrong when the United States remains the only major country on earth not to guarantee health care to every man, woman, and child as a right, not a privilege. They also understand that it is absurd that we pay almost twice as much per capita for health care as any other nation, including the highest prices in the world for prescription drugs, while our health care outcomes are often worse than other countries'.

Now, despite ferocious opposition from the insurance companies and the drug companies, poll after poll shows widespread support for a Medicare for All, single-payer program. A Reuters poll shows that over 70 percent of the American people, including more than half of Republicans, support Medicare for All. Interestingly, a few years ago, almost no candidates for office campaigned on

Medicare for All. Now a majority of Democratic candidates are strongly supporting that position and winning their elections.

Make no mistake about it. With Wall Street and the health care industry making hundreds of billions a year in profit from our current dysfunctional system, the fight for Medicare for All will require a monumental political struggle. But the very good news is that over the last three years, we have made enormous progress in that fight.

Now we have got to step up our organizing efforts. We have got to demand that any candidate we support has the guts to take on the insurance companies and the drug companies and support Medicare for All. We have got to bring doctors, nurses, patients, and businesspeople together into a broad coalition that helps lead the fight for universal health care. We need a national campaign, touching every city and town in the country, that proclaims loudly and clearly that health care is a human right. This is a fight we can win, and a fight we must win.

Nobody denies that we live in a highly competitive global economy. Nobody denies that for our country to succeed economically, we need to have the best-educated workforce in the world. Forty years ago, we did have the best-educated workforce in the world. Today that is no longer true. The world has changed, technology has changed, and our economy has changed. Our higher education system must change as well.

Unbelievably, each and every year, hundreds of thousands of bright young high school graduates are unable to get the higher education they need and deserve because their families lack the money. That is not only unfair to these young people but counterproductive to the well-being of the American economy. Further, millions of college graduates are trying to deal, year after year, with student debts of $50,000 or more.

When I campaigned on the need to make public colleges and universities tuition-free, I was once again met with a wall of opposition. How are you going to pay for it? What will this mean for private colleges? Should everybody who has the ability really be able to get a higher education?

While the politicians, pundits, and editorial boards were in opposition, it turned out that, every day, more and more Americans were agreeing with me. They understood that what I was calling for was not a radical idea. Not only did it exist in other countries around the world, but it used to exist in the United States. Fifty years ago, great public colleges and universities like the University of California, City University of New York, and other leading higher education institutions were tuition-free, or nearly so.

During the last several years, while support for making public colleges and universities tuition-free has soared, we have been making real progress on the ground. In cities and states throughout the country, mayors and governors have been moving in that direction. I was pleased to have personally attended events in New York State and San Francisco to help initiate programs that guarantee higher education to all, regardless of income.

And, by the way, according to the last three polls I have seen on this subject, over 60 percent of the American people now support making public colleges and universities tuition-free. They understand that if we can lower taxes on the wealthiest people in this country and the largest corporations, and if we can spend more on the military than the next ten nations combined, then, yes, we can make sure that every kid, regardless of income, gets the higher education he or she needs.

This is an issue that every American should support for the good of our country. It is an issue that young people, especially, should be all over. For the first time in the modern history of the United States, a sizable percentage of children will have a lower standard of living than their parents. That is unacceptable. Young people should not have to go deeply into debt to get the education they need for a middle-class career. If there is no other reason for the youth of America to be engaged politically, this should be it.

But, truth be told, there are many other reasons. Young people want and need meaningful and decent-paying jobs. They need affordable housing. They care deeply about combating climate change and creating a clean environment. They believe passionately in a woman's right to control her own body. They are in vigorous opposition to racism, sexism, homophobia, xenophobia, and religious intolerance.

The political reality of today is that a heavy percentage of older, more conservative people go to the polls. Young and progressive people tend to vote in much lower numbers. That has got to change. Young people are the future of this country. They need to stand up and fight for their future. They must get involved in the political struggle. Increasing voter turnout among young people must be a major priority of the progressive movement.

We're also making progress in criminal justice reform. Not fast enough, but we are moving forward. Several years ago, the abominations of our criminal justice system were not widely discussed. There were a handful of groups like Black Lives Matter, the ACLU, and others who were fighting hard to end a system that was racist and that criminalized poverty, but, by and large, that discussion had not yet reached mainstream political circles.

Well, because of strong progressive efforts, that's changed also. Today, for example, states all across the country now understand that the war on drugs has been a terrible failure. Many of these states are decriminalizing the use of marijuana or making it legal. Some communities are even beginning to expunge the records of people who were arrested for possession of marijuana.

But it's not just the war on drugs. There is a growing understanding about the insanity and injustice of a system that allows some 400,000 Americans to be in jail today, disproportionately people of color, without having been convicted of anything. They remain in jail because they are poor and cannot afford cash bail. In late August of 2018, the state of California became the first in the country to abolish bail as a condition of pretrial release. I have little doubt that other states will soon follow. This is an issue of elementary justice, and one we must vigorously pursue.

Today, there are prosecutors and district attorneys being elected who do not see their jobs as a mandate to send more and more people to jail. Rather, they want to reduce the prison population by finding constructive alternatives to incarceration. Further, many police departments are now training their officers to understand that lethal force should be the last response, not the first.

At a time when we continue to have more people in jail than any other country, an enormous amount of work remains to be done in creating a more just and humane criminal justice system. Progress, however, is being made and must be accelerated.

President Trump believes that he can score cheap political points by demonizing undocumented immigrants. He is not only on the wrong side of justice and decency; he is also in a very distinct minority. As a result of the hard work done by immigration reform groups and the progressive community, a strong majority of the American people now support comprehensive immigration reform and a path toward citizenship for the 10 million people in this country who are undocumented. Recent polls also show that some

80 percent of Americans support legal protection for the 1.8 million young people who are in DACA or eligible for the program.

I was extremely disappointed that Congress was unable to pass legislation that protected the young people in DACA from Trump's decision to end that program. Many of these people, who have lived in this country for virtually their entire lives, are now living in fear. The immigrant community is under fierce attack from the Trump administration. Even Hispanic Americans born here are being targeted—just for being nonwhite near the Mexican border—by having their passports taken away and deportation proceedings started. As progressives, we cannot turn our backs on them. Together, we must do what the American people want. We must pass comprehensive immigration reform.

The American people are beyond being shocked and disgusted at the incredible level of gun violence in this country. They want to do something about it. From a political point of view, this really is not a difficult issue. By overwhelming numbers, gun owners and non-gun owners want commonsense gun safety legislation. They want to improve the background check system. They want to put an end to the gun show loophole and the straw man provision that allows people who really should not have guns to buy them. Many of us want to ban the sale and distribution of assault weapons designed solely to kill human beings.

The American people want action on gun safety, but they are not getting it for one reason and one reason alone: the NRA. We need to learn a lesson from the brave students at Marjory Stoneman Douglas High School in Parkland, Florida, who stood up, fought back, and helped rally the nation. We need to support candidates for president and Congress who will represent the American people in gun safety legislation, not the NRA.

While the progressive agenda is gaining momentum, we've got

to continue expanding our vision and search for new ideas that address the needs of working families in a rapidly changing economy. In the wealthiest nation in the history of the world, every able-bodied person should have a decent-paying job. We can and should have a full-employment economy. Way back in 1944, President Franklin Delano Roosevelt talked about the right of every American to have a job. That was true then. It is true today.

A decent job not only provides a worker and his or her family with adequate income, but it does something more. It provides meaning in life. It enables one to be part of a community. Too many Americans today are falling through the cracks. They become alienated from society. They become destructive to others or self-destructive, turning to drugs, alcohol, or even suicide. What does it mean that in our country today life expectancy is actually going down? Guaranteeing a job for all will lower the crime rate, improve mental health, and create a stronger sense of community. It will create a much healthier and happier America.

A full-employment economy is not some wild utopian proposal. The truth is that in this country today there is an enormous amount of work to be done. We need millions of workers to rebuild our crumbling infrastructure—roads, bridges, water systems, waste-water plants, airports, rail, and affordable housing. At a time when our early childhood education system is totally inadequate, we need hundreds of thousands of workers to provide quality care to the young children of our country. As the nation ages, we will need many more workers to provide compassionate care to those who are reaching the end of their lives.

What should be clear to every political observer is that, today, we have a Republican president and Congress who, on issue after issue, are doing exactly the opposite of what the American people want. It really is pretty crazy.

The majority of Americans want health care for all. The Republican leadership wants to throw 32 million people off the health care they already have.

The Americans people want the wealthy and large, profitable corporations to start paying their fair share of taxes. The Republican leadership has provided billionaires and corporations with huge tax breaks.

The American people want to raise the minimum wage to a living wage. The Republican leadership wants to keep it at $7.25 an hour or even abolish the concept of the minimum wage altogether.

The American people want to make public colleges and universities tuition-free. The Republican leadership wants to cut federal Pell grants, making college even more unaffordable.

The American people want to expand Social Security benefits. The Republican leadership wants to cut them.

The American people want to protect *Roe v. Wade* and the right of a woman to have an abortion. The Republican leadership wants a Supreme Court justice who will end that protection.

The American people want to address the crisis of climate change, cut carbon emissions, and move toward sustainable energy. The Republican leadership does the bidding of the fossil fuel industry.

The American people want commonsense gun safety legislation. The Republican leadership offers thoughts and prayers.

The political revolution strives for the not-so-radical idea that we should have a government that represents all of the people, and not just the wealthy and powerful special interests. That goal will not be achieved unless we revitalize American democracy and bring millions more people into the political process. As we can see from today's situation in Washington, we cannot expect policies from government to represent working families if working people don't vote, are not involved in politics, and are not fighting for their rights. One of the great struggles that we must engage in is to do everything possible to increase voter turnout, especially among young people and lower-income Americans, because the more people that vote, the more progressives win.

Clearly, my right-wing Republican colleagues understand this reality as well as I do. That's why they pushed the Supreme Court to overturn important voter protections under the Voting Rights Act of 1965, and why Republican state officials are now aggressively pursuing voter suppression—making it harder for poor people, people of color, and young people to vote. Instead of wanting more people to be involved in our democracy, their entire "election reform" effort is to have fewer people vote. How's that for political cowardice.

Our job is not just to fight back against the voter suppression and extreme gerrymandering that are undermining the foundations of our democracy. We must move forward to universal voter registration. If you are eighteen years of age and an American citizen, you are registered to vote. End of discussion. No state can be allowed to deny anyone that basic democratic right. We must also make it easier for people to vote by moving Election Day to a weekend and increasing early voting opportunities. And we must end the outrage of millions not being able to vote, many of whom are people of color, even after they've served their time in jail for having committed a felony. We must strive for the United States to have one of the highest voter turnouts in the world, not one of the lowest.

In the United States, the essence of our democracy must be one person, one vote—not the amount of money you have. Billionaires should not be allowed to buy elections. Candidates should win elections based on their ideas and character, not by the size of their chief backers' bank accounts. The current campaign finance system is corrupt, and most Americans, regardless of their political views, understand that. Increasingly, as the costs of campaigns soar, we are seeing more and more "self-funders" running for office. These multimillionaires and billionaires are running for president, they are running for the Senate, they are running for the House and for governor. And those candidates who are not personally rich are increasingly dependent upon super PACs funded by the very wealthy.

The influence of money in our elections has always had a detrimental impact on our democracy. It is worse now. The disastrous 5–4 decision in *Citizens United* must be overturned, and we must move to the public funding of elections. We cannot allow a handful of very rich people to spend unlimited amounts of money to elect those who support their interests.

Over the last two years, Our Revolution, a number of other progressive organizations, and I have been working extremely hard to elect progressive candidates all across the country. And we've had a great deal of success—at the federal, state, and local levels.

While the election of Alexandria Ocasio-Cortez to Congress has received much attention, she is far from the only congressional victory we have achieved. In addition to Alexandria, strong young progressives like Rashida Tlaib, of Michigan, and Chuy García, of Illinois, were also elected in 2018. They will join Pramila Jayapal, of Washington, and Nanette Diaz Barragán, of California, who were elected in 2016 with the strong support of the progressive community. We are also hopeful that James Thompson, of Kansas, an excellent congressional candidate in a conservative area, can win his race.

In 2018 we have also made some extraordinary breakthroughs in gubernatorial races. Stacey Abrams of Georgia stands a chance to become not only the first Democratic governor of Georgia in sixteen years, but also the first black woman to ever become governor of any state. Ben Jealous of Maryland, a first-time candidate, shocked the entire Democratic political establishment in his state with his strong grassroots campaign and handily won his primary race. He is now in a tough fight to become governor of Maryland. Finally, Andrew Gillum pulled off a major upset in Florida, where, running as a strong progressive, he defeated one billionaire and three multimillionaires who heavily outspent him in the Democratic primary. The entire country is now watching to see whether he can defeat a Republican candidate endorsed by Trump.

In Pennsylvania, progressives pulled off another major upset with a victory by John Fetterman, mayor of Braddock, to become the Democratic candidate for lieutenant governor. John stands a good chance of winning the general election and becoming one of the political leaders in that state.

The truth is, however, that while the progressive movement has had good success at the congressional and gubernatorial level, our major achievement has been at the local level. As a result of a lot of hard work, Our Revolution has established over six hundred chapters, in almost every state in the country, and has brought hundreds of thousands of new people into the political process. From one end of this country to the other, including the most conservative areas, strong progressives have won dozens and dozens of races for school board, city council, county commission, state legislature, and other local offices.

Young people, working people, women, people of color, members of the LGBT community, people who a few years ago would never have given a moment's thought to becoming involved in electoral politics, are now running for office—and winning. Political barriers are being opened that will not be closed. This revitalization of American democracy is a beautiful sight to behold and has everything to do with the creation of a bright future for our country.

Real change and the fight for justice always begin at the grass-roots level. Real change takes place when ordinary people start questioning the status quo and ask, "Why not? Why can't we create a better society? Why can't we live in a world of economic, social, racial, and environmental justice?" And, at an unprecedented level in the modern history of our country, that is exactly what is happening.

As I write, the enormously important midterm elections will take place in two months. Like everyone else, I have no idea what the results will be. Will the Democrats gain control of the Senate? It's possible, but given the large number of seats they have to defend, it will be difficult. Will the Democrats, despite outrageous gerrymandering by Republican state legislatures, win a majority in the House? They have a real shot.

Regardless of what the election results may be, this I do know. I know that we are living at a pivotal moment in American history. It's a time in which millions of Americans have been left behind in a changing economy and many of them are living in despair. Amid vast wealth, the wages they earn are unlivable. Despite exploding medical technology, their health care is inadequate or nonexistent. At a time when most well-paying jobs require a higher education, their kids cannot afford to go to college.

These Americans believe, correctly, that much of the political and media establishment has ignored them and in many ways has held them in contempt. The very rich get much richer, and nobody much cares about them.

Our job, in the next two months, in the next two years, and into the future is to fight for a vibrant American democracy that resonates with love, hope, and prosperity. While Trump and his allies want to foment hatred and divisiveness—based on the color of our skin, our nation of origin, our religion, or our sexual orientation—our job is to bring people together. While Trump and his allies are pushing an agenda that benefits the wealthy and powerful, our job is to stand with the working people of our country and create a nation in which all Americans live in dignity and security.

The monumental struggle we are engaged in today is not just about our lives and our generation. It is about the kind of world we leave to our kids and grandchildren. In terms of climate change, it is about whether the planet we leave to them will even be healthy and habitable.

This is not a time for despair. This is not a time for depression. This is a time to stand up and fight back.

Please join us.

INDEX